AMERICAN IDENTITY AND THE MYTH OF POCAHONTAS

The Pocathontas Narratives in the Era of the Romantic Represantations of the Native Americans

MARIA S. B. BARBOSA

Mr. Wilson Publishing
New York

Copyright © 2014 – Barbosa, M.S.B..

1ˢᵗEedition – 2014

Cover: Camila Carbone

Cover Illustration: Hortêncio Bueno

Publisher: Mr. Wilson Publishing

The publisher is not liable for the concepts expressed by the author.

All rights reserved.

PERMISSIONS FROM THE AUTHOR FOR TRANSCRIPTION AND CITATION

Safeguarding the rights of the publisher, the author grants permission to use and transcribe excerpts of this work with prior written consent from the publisher and with appropriate citation of the source. The Publisher reserves the right to not allow any part of this work be copied, reproduced or transmitted by any means (electronic, photocopying, recording, or otherwise) without permission in writing from the publisher. Violators will be punished according to Law.

Barbosa, M.S.B., 1958 –
American Identity and the Myth of Pocahontas - 1ˢᵗ edition.
New York: Mr. Wilson Publishing
434 p. ; 6x9 in.
ISBN 13: 9780692290170 (paperback)
1. Literature. 2. American Literature. I. Title.
CDU: 821.111(73)

Printed in the USA

To Pocahontas, whose silence made me feel so uneasy that I had to find a way to make her talk.

CONTENTS

Preface 1

Introduction 3

Chapter 1 43

Historical Character / Literary Persona: Pathway of the Pocahontas Narratives from Colonial History to Romantic Literature

1.1. 46

Adventurers or Pilgrims? Historical and Literary Differences in the Early Colonization of Virginia and New England.

1.2. 76

From the Non-Pareil of Virginia to a long suffering Romantic Princess: the path of Pocahontas from a historical character to a fictional heroine.

1.3. 91

American Romanticism

1.4 111

From British Colony to Independent Nation: The Post-Revolutionary Period in the United States of America

Chapter 2 119

Explaining Theories: Crucial Views of Nation and National Identity, Miscegenation, Liminal Figures and Captivity Narratives

2.1. 121

Nation and National Identity

2.2. 132

Miscegenation

2.3. 157

Liminal Figures.

2.4. 168

Captivity Narratives

Chapter 3 181

Romantic Texts on Pocahontas and the construction of an American national Identity.

3.1. 184

"I might have forgotten that nature had put barriers between us": mixing races / mixing blood in Romantic narratives of Pocahontas

3.2. 246

Neither me, nor you, in between: Liminal figures in Romantic narratives on Pocahontas

3.3. 298

"Held as a hostage in the stranger's cell": Captivity Narratives in Romantic Texts on Pocahontas

Conclusion 348

Notes 364

Workes cited 389

Works consulted 420

PREFACE

Since the first time the story of Pocahontas appeared, it has always been focused on the supposedly and legendary rescue of John Smith and her marriage to a white colonist, although there are other far more outstanding historical debating issues regarding her story/history such as miscegenation, racial matters, and colonial growth.

The aim of *American Identity and the Myth of Pacohantas* is to go beyond that, and to show there is a more serious and lifelike outlook on that matter. The book fully analyses The Pocahontas Narratives in their historical, social and literary bases. It paves the readers' way by showing how these narratives had a crucial influence on the construction of an American national identity and, consequently, to the foundation of the new nation.

Maria Barbosa, with her literary engagement and responsibility, has always been aware of the role literature plays to provide information, and could not keep herself in silence while facing the importance of these narratives.

The book deals with a wide range of topics, from the development of the historical character of Pocahontas, how she secured an eminent place in early American history, and her path into a fictional heroic perspective; to fundamental issues as explaining theories that ground the concepts of, for instance, nation and national identity.

This very readable book devotes every chapter to a successful, elaborate analysis, which has proven important, useful and necessary to establish this intersection between the texts and the shaping of the American nation.

Francisca Oliveira
Professor at State University of Piauí

INTRODUCTION

Of the first settlers in Virginia, the most distinguished character was Captain Smith, a man who seemed to inherit every quality of a hero; a man of such bravery and conduct, that his actions would confer dignity on the page of the historian. With the life of this gallant colonist, the reader is admitted to so much knowledge of Indian manners, that this appears a very proper place to take a view of his adventures. But I have yet a stronger motive. With the history of Captain Smith is interwoven the story of Pocahontas, whose soft simplicity and innocence cannot but hold captive every mind; and this part of my volume, many of my fair readers will, I am persuaded, hug with the tenderest emotion to their bosoms.

John Davis [1]

Nations are historical constructs, as writers like Ernest Renan, in "What is a Nation?", Benedict Anderson in *Imagined Communities*, and Homi Bhabha in *The Location of Culture*, have argued. As Fernando Unzueta states in "Novel Subjects: on Reading and National (subject) Formation", nations can be regarded as artifacts "produced through a wide range of symbols, narratives, and discursive formations, including newspaper writing, history and literature" (75). In the process of building a nation, narratives are crucial to establish and argue that there are a history, a culture and a tradition from which that nation derives. Such a tradition, which may appear or claim to be old, is, as Eric Hobsbawm and Terence Ranger say in *The Invention of Tradition*, "often quite recent in origin and sometimes invented"(1). In relation to the construction of the American nation and the establishment of an American national identity, the need to establish a history is perceived in the relationship between the Anglo-Americans and Native Americans right after the American Revolution, when the establishment of a national identity was crucial to the very foundation of the new nation.

In *The Insistence of the Indian: Race and Nationalism in Nineteenth-century American Culture*, Susan Scheckel states that the USA's first attempts to forge a national identity coincided with the apparent need to define — and limit — the status and rights of Native Americans. These natives were, at the same time, actually displaced and literarily idealized, historically put outside the American nation and romantically entering American literature. Idealizations of Indians as the "first Americans" proved useful in developing a national identity distinct from Europe, but actual Native Americans were obstacles to the conquest of the continent. In the end, Native Americans occupied a troubled place in American society: marginalized and oppressed in reality, idealized or demonized in the imagination.[2] During the early decades of the nineteenth century, in a period Robert Tilton calls the "Era of the Romantic Indian" [3], the image of these natives circulated in different texts, as in the novels of James Fenimore Cooper, in the different plays with native themes, in captivity narratives, and in Black Hawk's autobiography.[4] Some of these texts are important sources of analysis for this book, as I explain below.

Cooper became famous for writing several novels dealing with the adventures of Nathaniel Bumppo in the so-called Leatherstocking series. His novels are considered American founding narratives, as stated by Richard Slotkin in *Regeneration through Violence: the Mythology of the American Frontier*, 1600-1860 (486-516).[5] In "Fenimore Cooper's America," Alan Taylor states that Cooper's novels of "frontier violence and adventure helped define the American experience and identity" (21), characterizing his novels as narratives that gave birth to the American nation. According to Doris Sommer, in *Foundational Fictions: the National Romances of Latin America*, a founding narrative is one that has, in a certain way, influenced the construction of a unique national identity, a kind of narrative that models the nation, as "identifiable as national anthems" (4).

Some of the plays dealing with the relationship between Native Americans and Europeans, which also appeared in the beginning of the nineteenth century, were about Pocahontas, who was portrayed in them as a princess who falls in love with a white man, thus helping him, sometimes against her own people. As Susan Scheckel argues, "calls for a national drama formed an important part of the project of American literary nationalism" (42), and the plays about Pocahontas were important for this project due to the mythical status her story had already achieved by that time. Pocahontas's story is also part of the captivity narratives that were widespread in the US even before the American Revolution. These are often first-person narratives in which the narrator tells about his/her experience as a prisoner among the natives. As Rebecca Blevins Faery states, in *Cartographies of Desire: Captivity, Race and Sex in the Shaping of an American Nation*, "[s]tories of Indian captivity are witness to the construction and operation of discourses of race in American" (10); they are, in this way, very important to the construction of an American national identity, especially because it is through these texts that the American view of the American environment and its original inhabitants, as well as their certainty about their own superiority, are ascertained.

All the texts mentioned above deal, in one way or another, with the anxieties and the cultural conflicts that surround the relationship between Native American and European. However, while Cooper's novels and Black Hawk's autobiography are centered on male figures, the plays about Pocahontas are centered on the female figure of the young native girl who had allegedly saved the life of the English adventurer John Smith.[6] In 1608, at the beginning of the British colonization in the US, John

Smith, one of the prominent men in the white settlement, was taken prisoner by the Algonquian people. He was then, according to his own account (*Generall Historie* 101), judged and condemned to death. Pocahontas, the daughter of the Algonquian chief Powhatan, pleaded for his life and rescued him. Some of the nineteenth century plays present a fictional adaptation of this rescue, with Pocahontas as the central character. One of the most famous captivity narratives is also centered on a female figure: Mrs. Mary Rowlandson's narrative of her own captivity among the Wampanoag during King Philip's War, a war between natives and English settlers from 1675 to 1676, the bloodiest conflict in seventeenth-century New England, temporarily devastating the frontier communities but eventually eradicating native resistance to the white man's westward thrust in that region (James D. Drake *King Philip's War* 1-2).

After these comments about some of the 19th century texts that deal with native themes, I have highlighted certain aspects: 1) the ways these texts portray the anxieties and conflicts between whites and Native Americans; 2) the possibility of relevant differences between male and female centered narratives in relation to these anxieties and conflicts; and 3) the possibility to include the narratives of Pocahontas among American founding narratives. These three questions are important to the development of this book because they are relevant to the narratives to be discussed. The anxieties and conflicts between white and Native Americans can be discussed in relation to the possibility of miscegenation and its consequences, a theme that is pervasive throughout the texts and that has stimulated much intellectual discussion and research, as in Tilton's Chapter I "Miscegenation and the Pocahontas Narrative in Colonial and Federalist America". In relation to female and male centered texts, it is also possible to see how they deal, in different ways, with the theme of miscegenation, as well as noting, in captivity narratives, that they acquire different connotations depending on the captive's race and gender. It is also possible to notice the different ways in which these texts portray liminal figures, like Pocahontas, who are present in both kinds of texts. Such portraits greatly differ depending on the race and gender of these figures. As for the possibility of including the narratives of Pocahontas among American founding texts, this is a crucial aspect of my work that is related to the themes present throughout nineteenth century narratives. Some of these narratives are analyzed in this book.

While liminal figures and captivity narratives are considered as literary categories of analysis, being widely discussed by literary critics in different texts and contexts, the issue of miscegenation is a historical one. However, due to the importance of this issue to the narratives about Pocahontas, it was necessary to include a discussion about it in this text.

As has been pointed out so far, questions like anxieties and conflicts, gender issues and founding narratives can be discussed in several of the Pocahontas narratives through three themes that are pervasive throughout the romantic texts about the Native American girl: 1) miscegenation and its consequences, because of her marriage to John Rolfe; 2) her role as a mediator in the relationship between her people and the white settlers; and 3) the captivity narratives inserted in them, first in relation to John Smith, who was a captive among the Algonquians, then in relation to Pocahontas herself, who was held captive by the white settlers of Jamestown. The main objective of this book is to show, through the analysis of these themes, that during the pre-Romantic and Romantic periods (1800-1860), the Romantic narratives of Pocahontas are important for the definition of an American national identity. In order to achieve this general objective, other minor aims were proposed: 1. To verify how some romantic narratives of different authors deal with the miscegenation, liminal figures and captivity among alien people[7] (natives as captive of whites or vice-versa) comparing them to the Pocahontas narratives; 2. To see if miscegenation issues, characters with mediator roles and captivity narratives inserted in romantic texts can help to ascertain how these texts deal with the concepts of nation and national identity; 3. To observe how these texts deal with aspects of cultural disparities and anxieties that were so frequent in pre-independent texts; 4. To establish whether the differences between male and female centered narratives have or have not influenced the construction of an American national identity. My hypothesis is that, even if the Pocahontas narratives do not deal with nation and national identity in the same way the other narratives do, they are important as a way of establishing an alternative view to what it means to be an American.

What makes a text a national founding narrative is not only its popularity, but also its inclusion in the school curriculum, as has happened to Cooper's novels. If none of the texts about Pocahontas has been entirely included in the curriculum, her story certainly has. As early as 1787, school books destined for American children had already included the story of Pocahontas as part of the national history, as, for instance, Noah Webster's *An American Selection of Lessons in Reading and Speaking* (1787), in which a chapter called "History of Pocahontas" is included.

Several books have been written about the Pocahontas episode, but none of them has really emphasized whether the narratives about the native girl have influenced the construction of an American national identity during Romanticism. Robert Tilton mentions the romantic texts, but his concern is with establishing the evolution of the American narrative from Smith's texts to post-civil war narratives, examining why her half-historic, half-legendary narratives so engaged the imagination of American people from the earliest days of the colonies through the conclusion of the Civil War. Rebecca Blevins Faery is concerned with the quest for a national identity;

however, her focus is not on the romantic period, but on Pocahontas's abduction, which she compares with Mrs. Rowlandson's captivity. In *Pocahontas and the Pilgrims: Rival Myths of American Origin*, Ann Uhry Abrams considers Pocahontas as a myth of origin, but she does not consider the romantic texts about Pocahontas as part of the romantic quest for a national identity in the period following independence. Susan Scheckel, on the other hand, deals with only two romantic plays, not mentioning other romantic texts on Pocahontas, like Lydia H. Sigourney's poem "Pocahontas" (1841) and John Davis's novel *Travels of Four Years and a Half in the United States of America during 1798, 1799, 1800, 1801, and 1802* (1803). She does not establish a close relationship between Pocahontas narratives and the texts of Cooper either. Neither Robert Tilton, nor Rebecca Blevins Faery, Susan Scheckel, or even Ann Uhry Abrams, have compared Romantic narratives of Pocahontas with James Fenimore Cooper's texts on the American frontier. Thus, it seems necessary to establish the place of the romantic narratives about Pocahontas alongside the founding narratives of Cooper, and to discuss their importance to the beginning of the American nation.

In order to attempt to achieve the objectives proposed and to establish the importance of the Pocahontas narratives to the construction of American national identity, this book focuses on the following romantic texts about Pocahontas: John Davis's novel *Travels of Four Years and a Half in the United States of America during 1798, 1799, 1800, 1801, and 1802* (1803); James Nelson Barker's play *The Indian Princess; or, La Belle Sauvage* (1808); George Washington Parke Custis's play *Pocahontas or the Settlers of Virginia* (1830); Lydia H. Sigourney's poem *Pocahontas and other poems* (1841); and Charlotte Mary Sanford Barnes's play *The Forest Princess or Two Centuries Ago* (1848). Other romantic texts to be discussed are: James Fenimore Cooper's novel *The Last of the Mohicans* (1826) and *The*

Pioneers (1823); Lydia Maria Child's novel *Hobomok* (1824); and Catherine Maria Sedgwick's novel *Hope Leslie* (1827).

Barker's and Custis's plays about Pocahontas were chosen because of their importance to the American popular drama of that period, while Barnes's play was chosen because her play, *The Forest Princess* (1848), was written as a response to the first two plays, Barker's *The Indian Princess* (1808) and Custis's *Pocahontas* (1830), which Barnes considered incorrect and historically inaccurate. An analysis of these texts will help to better understand the representation of the native girl in the romantic theater. Sigourney's seems to be one of the few widely appreciated poems about the "Indian Princess", thus the importance of including it in this analysis. Among the authors, only John Davis was not born in the USA, being a British citizen. However, Davis is considered, by most critics, as the first writer to have romanticized the relationship between Pocahontas and

John Smith, establishing a pattern that was followed by most writers afterwards. According to Tilton, it was Davis who first created the literary life of Pocahontas, focusing on her as the romantic heroine of a love story. Preposterous as they may be, as Carl Van Doren states in *The American Novel*, Davis's texts are interesting for being the first treatment of one of the most persistent of the American legends (20).

The other romantic texts were analyzed in order to establish differences and/or similarities between the narratives of Pocahontas and Cooper's founding narratives. The novels by Sedgwick, *Hope Leslie* (1827), and by Child, *Hobomok* (1824), which focus on fictional captivity narratives and white-Native American relationship, were useful in establishing the importance of the Pocahontas narratives since they deal with the anxieties and conflicts between European settlers and Native Americans that are present in the Pocahontas narratives.

When one thinks of Pocahontas, the first image that comes to mind is the figure of a pretty, grown up woman with long black hair and copper skin portrayed by the Disney Corporation in its 1995 released animation *Pocahontas*. However, the native girl called Pocahontas is not simply the protagonist of a Disney film. She lived in Virginia when the English settlers arrived there in 1607. Little is known of her life for certain, but Sharon Larkins, in "Using trade to teach about Pocahontas" (1988), establishes a chronological sketch of the crucial moments of her life, which is quoted by Tilton (7-8):

1. Her birth about 1595.
2. The traditional story of her rescue of Captain John Smith in 1607 and her continued relationship with him and help to the people of Jamestown.
3. Her abduction by Captain Argall in 1612 and subsequent captivity at Jamestown.
4. Her conversion to the Christian faith in 1613 while living in Jamestown.
5. Her marriage to John Rolfe in 1614 and the birth of her [their] son, Thomas, in 1615.
6. Her trip to England in 1616 including her success there as an Indian Princess.

[This would include her reception at the Court of King James I and Queen Anne, her attendance at The Vision of Delight, the Twelfth Night masque staged by Ben Jonson, and her sitting for the Simon Van de Passe engraving of her portrait, the only likeness of Pocahontas known to have been executed during her lifetime.]
7. Her death [and burial] at Gravesend in 1617.

William Strachey, in a 1612 travel narrative, *The Historie of Travaile Into Virginia Britannia*, states that Pocahontas had married an Algonquian private Captain called Kocoum after Smith's departure to England in 1609, when she stopped going to Jamestown. Such a marriage, however, was never confirmed, and Frances Mossiker, in *Pocahontas, the Life and the Legend* (1977), although discussing the possibility of its veracity, admits that all that is told about it is mere speculation, especially because Strachey is the only contemporary to report it (147).

Of all these facts, however, the most controversial, and, consequently, the one that has called the attention of most writers, is John Smith's rescue, for, while all the other contacts Pocahontas had with the white people had a white witness, the rescue had none. Her supposed marriage to a native private captain had no white witnesses either, but such an event had no influence in her relationship with the white settlers. One problem then is that the natives did not know how to write, thus being unable to record the event, and the Englishmen, who conquered the land, were the only ones with the power to narrate the story. As Edward Said states in *Reflections on Exile*, "history tends to be written from the point of view of the victor" (523). Thus, at that time, the only credible witness able to narrate the story and in writing is Smith himself. Nowadays, after so many analyses of colonial discourse have taught us to question official narratives, there are certainly increased doubts about whether the event — namely the rescue of John Smith — really happened. Another historical fact that leaves room for doubt is the fact that Smith only mentions the Pocahontas episode in his 1624 text, *The Generall Historie of Virginia, New England and the Summer Isles ...*, while, in his 1608 text, *A True Relation of Such Occurrences and Accidents of Noate as Hath Hapned in Virginia ...*, he tells how he was made prisoner by the Algonquians, without mentioning that his life was in danger at any time. Smith's revision of this historical episode is, according to Charles Larson, in his essay "Pocahontas Animated", the first example of a truly American narrative (12), a narrative that has been narrated and re-narrated throughout these last four centuries in different ways and through several media, from romantic to post-modern plays, novels, children's books, political speeches, poems, schoolbooks and films.

The first narratives about Pocahontas, beginning during her lifetime were totally centered on her as an important historical character. Books like Ralph Hamor's *A True Discourse of the Present State of Virginia (*1615) and William Strachey's *The Historie of Travaile Into*

Virginia Britannia, written in 1612 but published only in 1849, were presented by their authors as reporting the true facts about the history of the settlement of Virginia, and, consequently, of Pocahontas. After her death and till the end of the eighteenth century, several historians described the events in early Virginia, such as Robert Beverley in his book *The History and Present State of Virginia* (1705) and William Stith in his text *The History of the First Discovery and Settlement of Virginia* (1747). Even after the American Revolution she was still portrayed as an important historical figure, as in Jeremy Belknap's *American Biography* (1794) and William Robertson's *The History of America* (1796).

The historical Pocahontas assumes the form of a fictional character by the beginning of the nineteenth century, when the young British writer, John Davis, came to America and heard of her story. He found in it an extraordinary source for a romance, thus creating a literary life for her. He wrote four texts on the subject:

Farmer of New Jersey (1800), *Travels of Four Years and a Half in the United States of America during 1798, 1799, 1800, 1801, and 1802* (1803), *Captain Smith and Princess Pocahontas* (1805) and *The First Settlers of Virginia, An Historical Novel* (1806)[8].

From the nineteenth century on, the story of Pocahontas consists of a series of texts belonging to different genres — novels (*My Lady Pokahontas*, by John Esten Cooke, 1885; *Pocahontas: A Story of Virginia*, by John R Musick, 1895; *Pokahuntas: Maid of Jamestown*, by Anne Sanford Green, 1907; *The Story of Pocahontas*, by Shirley Graham, 1953); poems ("Pocahontas", by Bernard M. Carter, 1824; "The Forest Maiden." by William Gilmore Simms, 1833; *Pocahontas and Other Poems*, by Lydia H. Sigourney, 1841; *The Bridge*, by Hart Crane, (1930); biographies (*First Lady of America: A Romanticized Biography of Pocahontas*, by Leon Phillips, 1973; *Pocahontas, the life and the legend*, by Frances Mossiker, 1976); comics (*Pocahontas*, by the

Disney Corporation, 1995; *Young Pocahontas*, by Goodtime Entertainment, 1995); plays (*The Forest Princess*, by Charlotte Barnes, 1848; *Pocahontas. A Melo-Drama in Five Acts*, by S. H. Byers, 1875; *Pocahontas, a Burlesque Opera* by Welland. Hendrick, 1886; *The Origin of Necking: A Travesty on the Pocahontas-John Smith Episode* by Boyce Loving, 1932; *Princess Pocahontas and the Blue Spots*, by Monique Mojica, 1991); paintings (*Matoaka als Rebecca* by Simon Van de Passe, 1616; *Pocahontas* by Mary Woodbury, 1730; *The Baptism of Pocahontas*, by John Gatsby Chapman, 1840; *John Rolfe and Pocahontas* by James William Glass, 1850); children's books (*Pocahontas, A Princess of the Woods*, by Edward S. Ellis, 1907; *Pocahontas: Daughter of a Chief*, by Carol Greene, 1988; *My Name is Pocahontas*, by William Accorsi, 1992); sculptures ("Preservation of Captain Smith by Pocahontas", by Antonio Capellano, 1825; "Pocahontas", by Joseph Mozier, 1854; "Pocahontas of the Powhatans", by Griffin Chiles, 1993); CD-ROMs ("Young Pocahontas", by UAV, 1995), and so forth. Edward Gallagher, in "A Calendar of Pocahontas Materials", lists about seven hundred texts on Pocahontas and mentions the possibility of other three hundred and fifty texts that may also contain some reference to the native girl.

Each of these versions has added something to, or extracted something from, Smith's original text *Generall Historie* (1624), which can be seen as the primary source concerning this narrative. To Peter Hulme, in *Colonial Encounters: Europe and the native Caribbean, 1492–1797*, "the story of Pocahontas tells of an 'original' encounter of which no even passably 'immediate' account exists, a blank space which has not been allowed to remain empty" (138), the absence of any other reliable eyewitness being put into question and, therefore, the emergence of so many versions of this narrative throughout time. Tilton states that the Pocahontas narrative has "provided literary and visual artists with a flexible discourse that came to be used to address a number of racial, political and gender-related issues" (1). Not only written texts have been produced about Pocahontas, but also many different portraits of her have appeared, from Simon Van de Passe's "Matoaka als Rebecca", painted in 1616, while she was in London, to Disney's portrayal in 1995. It is important to remember that most of these literary and visual artists are white, and also that she was not able to write her own narrative. This way, the Pocahontas story has been narrated exclusively by white people.

Some critics, like Larson and Hulme, have questioned Pocahontas's lack of voice, stating that much has been said about her, but nothing by her. Hulme observes that "[n]one of Pocahontas words have come down to us directly, so we have no immediate access at all to what she might have thought of the strange patterns of events in which she was caught up" (146-47). Karen Robertson, in her essay "Pocahontas at the Masque", not only comments on the fact that Pocahontas did not produce her own narrative, but, also, that she could never voice her opinion on the documents written by Englishmen. Karen Robertson establishes some similarities between the behaviors of Pocahontas and John Smith, stating that "both were curious about another culture. Both crossed the ocean to see the powerful rulers of the opposing tribe" (557). However, there are two crucial asymmetries: Pocahontas could see both the rituals in her father's court and those of the court of James I, while Smith could see only the ritual of the Algonquians, for he had no access to the English court for not being of noble birth. For Robertson, the most important asymmetry, however, lies in the fact that Smith could tell his own story and produce his own narrative, while to Pocahontas such opportunity was denied, for "the process that converted Matoaka (her personal name) into Rebecca Rolfe did not include literacy" (558).

Not only Pocahontas's silence has been discussed

by the critics, but some critics like Ann Uhry Abrams, Leslie Fiedler, Peter Hulme, Rebecca Blevins Faery and Robert Tilton, have also studied the relationship between Pocahontas's and other important American narratives. Abrams compares the story of Pocahontas with that of the Puritan Founding Fathers, who certainly played a more vital role in the construction of an American national character, as is argued by Sacvan Bercovitch in *The Puritan Origins of the American Self*. To Abrams, these two narratives "embody the character of two diverse societies and often serve as rationales for their opposing ideologies" (xv). Abrams also establishes a crucial difference between the way these two narratives were constructed: in the loose history of Virginia, a shipload of single men founded Jamestown, and yet "Virginia's origin myth revolves around a female" (Pocahontas herself) (xv), while the Massachusetts narrative is centered on a patriarchal hierarchy, for the "nucleus of the Pilgrim migration was paternalistic and family oriented" (xv), with the heroes conducting a biblical style mission.

In *The Return of the Vanishing American*, Fiedler compares the narrative of Pocahontas to Hannah Dustan's story, which he sees as the true anti-Pocahontas. While the Pocahontas narrative embodies a possible reconciliation between white men and Native Americans, Hannah Dustan's story denies the possibility of miscegenation and "turns the weapon of the Indian against him in a final act of bloodshed and vengeance" (95). There are other critics such as Faery, who compare the story of Pocahontas as captive to white women's captivities; however, her focus is not on Hannah Dustan, but on Mary Rowlandson, a Puritan woman who was held captive by natives during King Philip's War. Tilton, on the other hand, compares the narratives of Pocahontas to Daniel Boone narratives in "their ability to express multiple and at times contradictory agendas" (1), for both narratives have served many different purposes. Daniel Boone's story, for example, was used to promote the westward expansion, while Pocahontas's story was used, for instance, as sectionalist propaganda[9].

Peter Hulme also compares the Pocahontas narrative to the Puritan narratives, and makes several comments on different historical accounts about the Native American girl, which he sees as ironic and incoherent, even though these accounts were obsessed with beginnings and coherence. He points out that the main difference between the two narratives of origin, Pocahontas's and the Puritans', resides in the fact that, while in Virginia a clear separation between English settlers and native peoples was established only after the massacre of 1622, in New England such a separation was established from the very beginning of the settlement. He argues that one of the Puritans' main objectives was "the establishment of a very clear division between civilization and savagery, between the 'city on the hill' and the alien and unregenerate force that lay beyond the pale" (139), which included sexual separation, while in Virginia interracial marriage was even allowed for a certain period, as a way of establishing a good relationship between the white settlers and the natives. The division between Europeans and natives only occurs when the latter notice that they were in danger of losing everything they had, for the white settlers were not visitors, but were there to stay. This awareness about the actual intentions of the European people led the Native Americans to attack Jamestown in 1622.

Two other aspects of Pocahontas's life have also been discussed by critics like Tilton and Hulme: her marriage to John Rolfe, which leads the critics to discuss the question of miscegenation, and her role as a mediator/liminal figure, which connects her story those of several other natives who had had the same role. Tilton argues that most of the romantic texts on Pocahontas emphasize the relationship between Pocahontas and John Smith instead of her marriage to John Rolfe, due to the fear of miscegenation, which confirms Fiedler's view in comparing Pocahontas to Hannah Dustan.

Pocahontas's role as a mediator between her culture and the Europeans' is discussed by Peter Hulme, who points out the importance of liminal figures at that crucial historical moment, since they played a vital role to the survival of colonies like Virginia. Such intermediaries were considered "cultural half-breeds inhabiting that dangerous no-man's land between identifiable cultural positions, and therefore seen as inherently suspicious and potentially dangerous translators who might quite literally be traducers, crossing cultural boundaries only to double-cross their king and country" (142). Several of these mediators during the colonial period were, at one time or another, suspects of treachery. Pocahontas, however, apparently was not perceived as occupying a dangerous position, for none of her biographers mention this possibility. A possible explanation for this view is that Pocahontas performs the first successful crossing from native to English culture in Virginia, while before her, as critics like Peter Hulme and Robert Tilton point out, all the crossings which can be historically documented are the other way around: white settlers who are said to have joined the native people in order to survive. However, this kind of crossing was, to the white settlers, unacceptable, and so, they celebrated Pocahontas's crossing as a proof of their superiority.[10]

Lately, with the release of the Disney animation, discussions on the Pocahontas story have started all over again — and also the discussion of the animation as it can be compared to Smith's text. There is one point of agreement among different critics: there are many discrepancies between Smith's narrative and Disney's version. It is interesting to notice that, in spite of these discrepancies, or maybe because of them, the release of the Disney animation made many more people become interested in the Pocahontas narratives, for the number of critical texts dealing with Disney's version in contrast with the older narratives is astonishing; to mention just a few: Elizabeth Cook-Lynn's "American Indian

Intellectualism and the New Indian Story (Writing about American Indians)" (*Natives and Academics Researching and Writing about American Indians*, edited by Devon A. Mihesuah); Amy Aidman's "Disney's Pocahontas: Conversations with Native American and Euro-American Girls" (*Growing Up Girls: Popular Culture and the Construction of Identity*, edited by Sharon R. Mazzarella and Norma Odom Pecora); Joni Adamson Clarke's "A Captive of History" (*Women's Review of Books*; 9/1/1995); Tom Geir's "Inventing a Princess" (*U.S. News & World Report*; 6/19/1995); and many others.

What this introduction has shown, so far, is that much has been written about Pocahontas, the historical character, and also about some fictional texts in which she is the main character. However, none of them has established any kind of relationship between the romantic narratives on Pocahontas and the other romantic texts that are considered important foundational narratives of the American nation. This is a "blank space" that has not yet been fulfilled, and it is to such fulfillment that this text has tried to contribute.

In order to write this book, the following steps were necessary: first, a comparison between the narratives on Pocahontas and the other narratives was made. Then, such a comparison was analyzed so that common and/or contrasting elements were highlighted. Finally, in a second analysis, such elements were discussed according to the theories of nation and national identity. This research dealt with different kinds of sources, from books, journals, newspapers, magazines, and legal documents, all of them serving a specific purpose: to clarify the points under discussion and to open other possibilities of research.

Although Pocahontas is not only a fictional character, but was also an actual human being, the discussion of historical accuracies and/or inaccuracies in the texts to be discussed is not part of the scope of this book. Thus, the figure of the native girl was treated, throughout this research, as a fictional character just like all the other romantic characters that were compared to her, as a constitutive element of the basis of narratives of national American identity. However, due to its importance, John Smith's was used as a proto-narrative and as a basis for all other narratives. Proto-narrative is defined, according to Eric Gans, in "Originary Narrative", as the most ancient narrative which concerns the theme, the text that gave origin to all others (7), in this case the very basis for the Pocahontas narratives, either historical or fictional.

This book is composed of five chapters, including the introduction and the final conclusion:

1. Historical Character / Literary Persona: Pathway of the Pocahontas Narratives from Colonial History to Romantic Literature.

This chapter discusses the differences between the settlements of Virginia and New England. Such differences can explain the reasons why the Pocahontas narratives have changed from historical to literary ones. There are also some comments on the post-revolutionary period in the USA, as well as about the 1812-war and its importance to the establishment and/or reinforcement of an American national identity Such comments lead to a discussion of American Romanticism and its importance to building an American nation.

2. Explaining Theories: Crucial Concepts on Nation, Miscegenation, Liminal Figures, and Captivity Narratives.

This chapter deals with the theories that support this discussion, such as the theories on Nation and Nationalism, which are explained and connected to the theories about national and cultural identity. Theories about miscegenation, liminal figures and captivity narratives are also discussed, always having in mind the building of an American national identity during Romanticism — a period in which some of the Pocahontas narratives are accepted by a general public.

3. Romantic Texts on Pocahontas and the

Construction of an American National Identity.

It constitutes the analysis of the romantic texts in themselves, and is formed by three sections:

3.1. "I might have forgotten that nature had put barriers between us": Mixing Races / Mixing Blood in Romantic Narratives of Pocahontas.

This section presents a discussion about gender and race relationship and the question of miscegenation in the construction of an American national identity during Romanticism. There is a brief description of how the perception of Native Americans changed from the beginning of colonization to the beginning of the nineteenth century when they were perceived as racially inferior, thus justifying the different ways of portraying interracial marriage in the romantic texts of Pocahontas as well as in James Fenimore Cooper's, Lydia Maria Child's and Catherine Maria Sedgwick's texts.

3.2. Neither me, nor you, in between: Liminal Figures in Romantic Narratives on Pocahontas.

This section deals with the role of mediator figures and the relationship between European people of different origins, always keeping in mind the quest for a national identity. There is a brief discussion on the importance of cultural brokers as well as on the different kinds of liminal figures portrayed in romantic texts, besides some comments about historical characters who played crucial roles during the colonization process.

3.3. "Held as a hostage in the stranger's cell": Captivity Narratives in Romantic Narratives on Pocahontas.

In this sub-chapter, there is a discussion about the captivity episodes inserted in some of the texts, and their importance to the construction of a national identity. There is a brief discussion of actual captivity narratives in order to better understand how Pocahontas's captivity is inserted in narratives about her as well as the different ways of portraying it in romantic texts either on Pocahontas or on any other Native American girl.

Finally, the Conclusion points out the importance of the Pocahontas narratives to the establishment of an American national identity and presents suggestions for further research. It must be said at the beginning that the wealth of available material for such a project is enormous. Therefore, a total coverage would be impossible. My objective is not to be exhaustive, but to show that, besides the foundational narratives of James Fennimore Cooper, the Pocahontas narratives have also played a crucial role in the formation of an American national identity within the Romantic Period.

1

HISTORICAL CHARACTER / LITERARY PERSONA: PATHWAY OF THE POCAHONTAS NARRATIVES FROM COLONIAL HISTORY TO ROMANTIC LITERATURE

It is almost certain that if there had been no Jamestown, there would have been no Plymouth.

Thomas J. Wertenbaker [1]

All that part of the northern American continent now under the dominion of the king of Great Britain, and stretching quite as far as the cape of Florida, went at first under the general name of Virginia

William Byrd [2]

Emory Elliot, in "New England Puritan Literature", states that "[a]s many historians admit, a record of past events is the hybrid product of facts and interpretation" (205). Hayden White, in *Tropics of Discourse*, suggests that a historical situation can be configured according to the historian's wish to emphasize a certain aspect, or to endow a certain event with a particular meaning. This is, as White says, "essentially a literary, that is to say fiction-making, operation" (85). This connection between History and Literature is very pertinent to this dissertation, since it deals with historical and literary characters and texts. When a historical event changes into a literary one, being fictionalized and thus entering the fictional world, it still keeps its historical aspect, acquiring thus a different status, a kind of mythical, legendary one. This is what has happened to Pocahontas: when she enters the literary field through John Davis's hands, her story acquires a legendary feature, and becomes open to different interpretations and transformations, not belonging solely to history, but to the world of the imagination.

This chapter aims to situate the narratives of Pocahontas within the literary history of the USA from the colonial period to 1855, when American Romanticism was at its apex. Such narratives, some considered historical, some fictional, which may have had different interpretations throughout these last four centuries, show how history and literature are intermingled in literary texts that deal with a historical character like the Native American girl, Pocahontas.

1.1. ADVENTURERS OR PILGRIMS? HISTORICAL AND LITERARY DIFFERENCES IN THE EARLY COLONIZATION OF VIRGINIA AND NEW ENGLAND.

The early histories of colonial New England and Virginia present many similarities, yet differ in important aspects. The colonists traveled to these two regions for a variety of reasons in the early 1600s. The differing motivations led to the development of unique societies in each colony. Such differences help explain why the Pocahontas narratives assume literary importance only in the beginning of the nineteenth century, while the Puritan narratives achieved a very important status from the very beginning. Furthermore, these Puritan narratives, like the texts of William Bradford, History of Plymouth Plantation (1650), Mrs. Rowlandson, A Narrative of the Captivity and Restoration of Mrs. Mary Rowlandson (1682) and Cotton Mather, Magnalia Christi Americana (1702), paved the way to the narratives of James Fenimore

Cooper, thus helping to establish the "normative American romance" (Giddens 2000). Since one of the main objectives of this dissertation is to show the importance of the Pocahontas narratives for the construction of a national American identity, it is necessary to explain the differences between the first two English settlements in what is now the USA.

In her article "The Architecture of New England and the Southern Colonies as it Reflects the Changes in Colonial Life" (1978), Valerie Ann Polino states that

> Between the two strong and opposing cultures of Virginia and New England, the only continuous highway was the sea. The early model of New England could hardly have worked in the South, and neither could the early model of Virginia have worked in the North. Two main cultures emerged from the English settlements in the North and South: the Southern planter society had a ruling aristocracy and great class distinctions between the wealthy and the poor; New England was more of an egalitarian settlement under the control of a Puritan oligarchy, in which a strong middle class had developed. (2)

Both the South and the North, however, had a point in common: they had to establish a relationship with the American wilderness and especially with the people who lived in it, the Native-Americans. Nevertheless, since the very beginning of the process of the European colonization in the USA one of the strongest differences between the settlers in Virginia and New England was the ways in which they established such a relationship. And this difference starts even before the beginning of the colonization, due to the different views of the natives of the Americas already discussed in European discourse.

As Alden T. Vaughan, in "Sir Walter Ralegh's Indian Interpreters, 1584-1618" states, after Christopher Columbus's voyages, the European imaginary was full of the images brought by the Spanish settlers through letters, travel writings, and, more importantly, through the artifacts taken to Europe by the travelers. But nothing impressed the European imagination during the late fifteenth century through the beginning of seventeenth century more than the existence of Native Americans, for the very idea of their existence caused a great surprise in the so-called Old World. When the English, under the rule of Elizabeth I, finally decided to establish themselves in a colony in the New World, a hundred years behind the Spaniards, many stories about the natives had already been told in Europe, and their reputation as treacherous, cruel, cannibals was well established. According to Andrew MacDonald and Mary Ann Sheridan, in Shape-shifting: Images of Native Americans in Recent Popular Fiction, "since the first encounters of pre-colonial times, Europeans have shaped, changed, and distorted the indigenous people to serve white people's needs" (xi). Thus, when the Susan Constant, the Godspeed and the Discovery docked in Chesapeake Bay on May 13, 1607, the people who came in them had already made up their minds about the natives they expected to meet, especially after the failure of the Roanoke Island colony, founded by Sir Walter Raleigh, which mysteriously vanished with no trace except for the word "Croatoan" scrawled on a nearby tree.

The Powhatans, who lived in Chesapeake Bay, had already had some contact with European people. Although there is no actual evidence of their involvement in the disappearance of the Roanoke colony, some writers like France Mossiker suggest that they may have cooperated with the Algonquian-speaking neighboring tribes in an attack on that colony (35). However, their first contact with the settlers at Jamestown was amiable, without actual threats or violence, except for some isolated acts. The colonists, most of them adventurers who were not prepared for the colonial enterprise, found soon enough that they needed the natives' help to survive. Thus, as Peter Hulme says, a friendly relationship between the settlers and the natives was somehow established, especially after the marriage of Pocahontas with the tobacco planter John Rolfe (141-142). That peace ended only in 1622, with the Jamestown massacre led by

Pocahontas's uncle Opechancanough. Only after this event did the reality of the colonization process seem to fit the previous idea Europeans had formed of the natives as treacherous and cruel. The fact that the natives had been protecting their land was not taken into account.

Peter Hulme calls the period from 1607 to 1622 the "pre-history of Virginia", a moment when Native Americans received the strangers in a friendly way, trying even to initiate them into their own customs, as in the case of John Smith, whose "rescue" was probably a ritual of incorporation, in which he was given a gift, Powhatan's dearest daughter Pocahontas. Hulme describes this kind of native behavior in terms of "reciprocity", a system similar to "compadrazgo", in which strong enemies were included as members of the nation by sponsoring a native, something that the English people could not understand. To support his view, Hulme uses Pocahontas's last reported words, written by John Smith in the second version of his own history without a single comment. This absence of comments is what makes Hulme question the meaning of her words, and try to make sense of them in order to understand Pocahontas's behavior as well as her people's customs (Hulme 146-151).

Here is how John Smith, in *Generall Historie* (1624), describes his last encounter with Pocahontas, and her last reported words:

> hearing shee was at Branford with diuers of my friends, I went to see her: After a modest salutation, without any word, she turned about, obscured her face, as not seeming well contented; and in that humour her husband, with diuers others, we all left her two or three hours, repenting my selfe to haue writ she could speake English. But not long after, she began to talke, and remembred mee well what courtesies shee had done: saying, *You did promise Powhatan what was yours should bee his, and he the like to you; you called him father being in his land a stranger and by the same reason so must I doe you*: which though I would haue excused, I durst not allow of that title, because she was a King's daughter; with a well set countenance she said, *Were you not afraid to come into my father Countrie, and caused feare in him and all his people (but mee) and feare you here I should call you father; I tell you then I will, and you shall call me childe, and so I will bee foreeuer and euer your Countrieman. They did tell vs alwaies*

> *you were dead, and I knwe no other till I came to Plimoth; yet Powhatan did command Vttamatomakkin to seeke you, and know the truth, because your Countriemen will lie much.* (238-39, my emphasis)

Such a dialogue happened when John Smith visited Pocahontas in Branford, England, where she was living with her English husband. His lack of understanding is clear, for he interrupts his description of his visit, and he does not comment on the fact that she recriminates him and his fellowmen for lying to her. He does not even justify himself for having lied to her, and this is further indication of his lack of comprehension. As Hulme says, Pocahontas's last words "clearly make no sense at all to John Smith, and yet had so impressed him as a statement of Pocahontas's opinion that he quotes them without further comment" (147).

Hulme also states that when the natives perceived the visitors were not visitors, but invaders who were there to stay and to demand more and more land, they decided it was time to expel them. The massacre of 1622 is the result of such a decision, when the natives, led by Pocahontas's uncle, Opechancanough, killed most of the white people in Jamestown. This massacre is, in Hulme's view, a turning point in the history of the Virginia colony, the real beginning of its history. From then on, says Hulme, Europeans could see the natives the way they had always wanted to see them: as treacherous, savage, unreliable, incoherent. From this moment on, one can say that the writings already existent about the natives and the natives' real behavior finally coincide. There is, thus, a paradox here: the English people, who were the strangers in Virginia, are seen as the rightful owners of the land, while the natives are seen as their oppressors (Hulme 157-158).

In New England, the settlers were much better prepared to deal with the land, and did not need the natives' help to survive. From the moment the Mayflower arrived, the British, who saw themselves as the chosen people coming to the Promised Land, established a clear distinction between themselves and the natives. As Hulme points out, there is a non-native/ideological coherence in New England lacking in the Virginia settlement: from the very beginning of their settlement, the Puritans in the Massachusetts Bay established a clear difference between themselves, the "chosen people", and the natives, the "savages". They inscribed themselves in what they had heard and read about the natives in Europe and did not allow any close contact (Hulme 139).

Sacvan Bercovitch establishes a series of important concepts about what it was to be a Puritan at that historical moment. The main concept is certainly the notion of New England as the Elected Nation while the Pilgrims were seen as the chosen people themselves. The Puritan writers saw themselves in the wilderness as the people of God and thought that all obstacles they would face would be sent by Satan to prevent them from establishing a city on the hill, a perfect Christendom. They all had an eschatological consciousness which made them firmly believe that their personal, as well as national destiny, was to serve as an example to the world (Bercovitch 72-74).

The differences between the settlements of Virginia and New England are not restricted to the way the settlers dealt with the natives. The settlers themselves were quite different. Like most European ventures to the Americas, the English venture to Virginia was largely dominated by men in its early years. All of the 104 settlers who sailed up the River James in 1607 were men. The initial group had a great number of wealthy adventurers, some artisans, and only a small number of agricultural laborers whose practical skill might have helped the inexperienced settlement survive the first winter. As Kathleen M. Brown points out, in her essay "Women in Early Jamestown", "[t]he maleness of the landing party at Jamestown and the overwhelmingly male character of the settlement in subsequent years had a huge impact on relations with local Native Americans" (4).

Brown also argues that the small numbers of

English women appear to have given Powhatan hopes that the strangers could be absorbed into his chiefdom through adoption, hospitality, and the provision of food, probably because he was already aware of the European war technology, much more developed than his own, and to make them partners would be helpful in dealing with his nation's enemies. Powhatan probably planed the capture and confinement of English commander John Smith in 1608, which concluded with a ritual of execution, apparently stopped by Powhatan's daughter, Pocahontas. John Smith claimed that the Native American girl had saved his life and years later wrote a report of her intercession, a fact that became known as the starting point for the Pocahontas legend. Powhatan also attempted to construct a father-son relationship with John Smith, reminding him of the privileges and obligations such a relationship conferred upon him. Possibly, Brown goes on, Powhatan also permitted the distraction provided by Pocahontas's retinue of women, in which young women adorned in ritual pocones (red paint) crowded John Smith, crying "Love you not mee." As long as the English stayed inside the protective palisade at Jamestown and Powhatan hoped to incorporate them peacefully, war could be avoided. When individuals left the fort, however, they were subject to the strategies of local werowances, which included female werowances like Oppossunoquonuske using the possibility of sexual pleasure to attract defenseless English men into a trap (3).[3]

In the Virginia settlement, the imbalanced sex ratio and the need for skilled agricultural laboring men left the English ill-prepared to deal with the day-to-day demands of a new settlement. This weakness also contributed significantly to Anglo-Native American relations, motivating the English community to negotiate, trade, or raid for the foodstuffs they so urgently needed. Soon after Captain John Smith returned to England to be treated for an injury, in 1609, the settlement endured a winter of hunger and death. Having failed to plant or accumulate enough grain for their needs and wanting supplies from England, the five hundred person settlement became desperate for food: they were, as John Smith tells it,

> most miserable and poore creatures; and those were preserved for the most part, by roots, herbes, acornes, walnuts, berries, now and then a little fish: ... yea, even the very skinnes of our horses. Nay, so great was our famine, that a Salvage we slew, and buried, the poorer sort tooke him up againe and eat him, and so did divers one another boyled and stewed with roots and herbs: And one amongst the rest did kill his wife, powdered her, and had eaten part of her before it was knowne, for which hee was executed, as hee well deserved. (John Smith *Generall Historie* 204-205)

Even though the Council later claimed that the man had murdered out of hatred, not hunger, word of the cannibalism spread, provoking John Smith to mention ironically that the dish "powdered [salted or flour-dredged] wife" was unknown to him (*Generall Historie* 205).

Disease also claimed many lives, as the estuarial situation and disruptive habits of settlers combined to turn the water into a harmful brew. Under John Smith, settlers risked Native American violence to live at a healthier distance from Jamestown. Following John Smith's return to England, however, settlers returned to the fort and its damaging conditions, increasing the death rate from disease.

The suffering within Jamestown during its first decade corresponded with a weakening of the relations between Native Americans and Europeans. One of the central misunderstandings concerned the Native American provision of corn to the English. Powhatan may have expected to get advantage of the English anxiety for food to ascertain his people's domination, but the English viewed native corn as ready for apprehension if it was not given without restraint. It is John Smith who says so:

> In the interim we began to cut in peeces their Canowes, and they presently to lay downe their bowes, making signes of peace: peace we told them we would accept, would they bring us their Kings bowes and arrowes, with a chayne of pearle; and when we came againe give us foure hundred baskets full of Corne, otherwise we would break all their boats, and burne their houses, and corne, and all they had. (*Generall Historie* 136)

One wonders, too, whether the fact that native women produced the vast quantities of corn, which was stored for winter use, did not add to the anger of the English at their complete dependence upon "savages". English chroniclers of native life, reluctant or unable to identify the irony of the failure of their own "civilized" method of agricultural production, undoubtedly spilled much ink in describing the task of agricultural work by native women. Beginning in 1609, soon after John Smith's departure, Jamestown was mostly at war with Powhatan, forcing the re-entrenchment of colonists inside the fort. The kidnapping of Pocahontas and her subsequent marriage to John Rolfe sealed the peace, but it seems that, after it, Powhatan was not interested in incorporating the British any more, even refusing to marry another of his daughters to Sir Thomas Dale. As Mossiker argues, "the English governor must content himself with one Powhatan princess; in Pocahontas, he already had his pledge of peace" (197).

As for the colonists in New England, when the Mayflower docked there on May 13th, 1620, they had totally different ideas on their minds from the settlers in Jamestown. They were mostly Puritans who had migrated to Holland in order to escape religious persecution, but, unhappy about living in a foreign country where they could neither use their own language nor follow their own customs, decided to move on to a place where they could live according to their own beliefs and using their own language: the so called New World.

According to Henry M. Ward, in *The United Colonies of New England*, it was through the friendship and support of Sir Edwin Sandys and others that the Puritans saved money and acquired a small vessel, the Speedwell, hired another, the Mayflower, and decided to cross the wide waters to the northern part of America, where they should worship God in their own way and still be Englishmen. Having secured a grant from the Virginia Company to settle in the Hudson Valley, and a promise from the king that he would not interfere with them, and having mortgaged themselves to a company of London merchants, they set forth with heroic hearts to run into the unfamiliar perils of the sea and of the wilderness. The Speedwell proved not to be seaworthy, and the little band re-embarked from Plymouth, England, on the Mayflower alone. Their minister Robinson had stayed in Leyden, and Brewster was the leader. He and John Carver were well advanced in years, but most of the people were in the prime of life. William Bradford was thirty and Edward Winslow was twenty-five. They came to the New World with their families, unlike the colonists in Virginia (Ward 21).

In *Warpaths: Invasions of North America*, Ian K. Steele states that the great Puritan migration was yet to begin, and as a great quantity of Puritans were ready to join the colony, it was considered far more reasonable to have a royal charter than a mere land grant. A charter was therefore secured from Charles I in March, 1629, confirming the land grant of 1628, namely, from three miles south of the Charles River to a point three miles north of the Merrimac, extending westward to the Pacific Ocean which was believed to be much nearer than it is. This new company was styled the Governor and Company of Massachusetts Bay in New England. The government was to be placed in the hands of a governor, deputy governor, and eighteen assistants, to be elected annually by the company. This charter increased the difference between the colony in Virginia and the colony in the Massachusetts Bay: although very similar to the 1612-charter of Virginia, it differed in the sense that New England was to be ruled from the colony itself, while the 1612-charter determined that Virginia should be ruled from England, where the Governor would have his seat. This certainly gave a freedom to the New Englanders that the Virginians did not have, and, this fact, together with all the aspects already discussed, helped establish the way literature would develop in each colony (Steele 85-86).

Because Virginia and New England had different beginnings, they also had different developments in literature.

The greatest difference between Virginia and New England in relation to their initial histories and literatures derives from the fact that Virginia developed into a rural colony and, as Robert Spiller says, in *The Literary History of the United States*, the "lack of towns was also a serious deterrent in the south to the development of literary activities" (16). It is obvious that farmers can develop a literature, but, as Spiller also states, "sustained literary production is a characteristic of urban rather than rural environment" (16). This emphasis on the rural areas in the South, together with the lack of printing houses till the middle of the eighteenth century, made it possible to the Northern colonies to have a better developed literature during the colonial period. This does not mean that Virginians did not write or read, but that their writings were published in Europe, instead of in Virginia itself, and also that the first readers were Europeans, who were curious to know about the colonies but who were not aware of the hardship of the settlers' lives. So, directed to Europe and European readers, the writings from Virginia did not deal with daily life activities or educational devices as the writings from New England did.

It is possible to see, then, how historical differences in the colonization processes of Virginia and New England interfered in the construction of different colonial literatures, with different concerns. In other words, while the Puritan narratives were, from the very beginning, trying to build a different collective identity, such was not the case of the Pocahontas narratives, which only acquired that status during the early nineteenth century when, as Renata Wasserman points out, in her *Exotic Nations*, American writers like James Fenimore Cooper in the novel *The Pioneers* (1823) started to use an Europeanized image of the Native American as exotic as it was established by European writers like Bernardin de Saint

Pierre in *Paul and Virginie* (1788) and Chateaubriand in *Atala* (1808). It is possible to say that Catharine Maria Sedgwick, in her novel *Hope Leslie* (1827), has also made the same use of this image. Before the 1776-war of Independence, writers from the Southern colonies had European readers in mind. As Richard Slotkin points out, the South's "literary roots were in London rather than in the New World" (213). While literature was a pervasive presence in New England, with the first press being founded right at the beginning of its colonization (1640), in the South there were fewer presses and fewer readers. It was not surprising that Southern writers would have their texts circulating only in manuscript in the upper circle of Virginia society by the end of the 18th century, right before the Revolution (Slotkin 213-214). All the Pocahontas narratives written during the colonial period were thus printed in Europe, like the narratives of John Smith, Robert Beverley, and William Robertson, while the New Englanders' texts were already printed in

America, having the settlers as their primary readers, such as the texts of John Winthrop, Cotton Mather and Increase Mather.[4]

Two books were of great importance in the accounts of the colonization of New England: William Bradford's *Of Plymouth Plantation* and John Winthrop's *The History of New England from 1630 to 1649*. In these journals, the authors narrated the events they witnessed, not only the successes, but principally their failures, which are, strangely enough, their very success: they were able to face dangerous nature and hostile environment, to deal with the Native Americans, and to develop an economy. However, in the eyes of a Puritan, they failed for not returning to the lost purity of earlier times, for they believed at first that going to America was like going to an earthly paradise where Europeans would regain the innocence of the first times, as described in the Bible, before Adam's fall. Even though admitting they failed, they insisted on writing themselves a central role in the sacred drama they thought God had designed for man in America. They were, in fact, as Richard Ruland and Malcolm Bradbury state, in *From Puritanism to Postmodernism*, trying to found a new nation "based on a new covenant of men and a new relation of religion and law" (14). The Puritan writer had a hard task: to displace the center, which was in Europe, to direct it to the small group of pilgrims who had accepted God's will and to establish Christendom in the wilderness. Although using the so called "plain style", the Puritan writings are full of metaphors and typology, and the main form of these writings, besides the historical narratives, are the sermons, which were vital to the community, for they were closely linked to life in the Puritan congregation, where the minister was a key figure. The sermons, which had the purpose of generating emotion and faith, were used as effective discourse, becoming, as time went by, important instruments to call people to repentance and salvation.

These Puritan texts served as the basis for several

other writings in American literature, and can be considered as the most influential text from the colonial period. Many of the writers who produced great literary works afterwards, like Nathaniel Hawthorne and Herman Melville, were clearly influenced by the Puritans' way of writing, with their metaphors and typology. According to Donna M Campbell, in "Puritan Typology", typology is "the interpretation of Old Testament events, persons, and ceremonies as signs which prefigured Christ's fulfillment and new covenant with the apostolic church" (1). This kind of interpretation is clearly noticed in the Puritan writings, and they have influenced many other writers, like James Fenimore Cooper, Catherine Maria Sedgwick and Lydia Maria Child, whose texts come from the Puritan tradition. Thus, it is important to understand how Puritan literature developed in order to better understand nineteenth century novels that, although with very different themes, also deal with important Puritan ideas, like the need of salvation and the danger of damnation due to the contact with Native American people. Cotton Mather's texts *Wonders of the Invisible World* (1689) is a good example of Puritan narratives with themes like damnation and salvation. In this text he defends both belief in witchcraft as an evil magical power, and Mather's own role in the witchhunt conducted in Salem, Massachusetts. The worst sin to a Puritan would be sexual intercourse with a native, a fear that is clearly portrayed in some of the nineteenth century texts that are discussed in Chapter 3.

Besides historical texts and the sermon, which were public texts, the Puritans also had the personal ones, the journals, diaries and letters. The latter allows us to understand Puritan domestic life. The central expressions of the American Puritan mind were far from the imaginative literature, but such expressions had their own metaphysical and allegorical resources that influenced much of later American Literature. Some literary genres were not allowed, like the theater; others, like poetry, had a very determined place; and prose fiction was not trusted. But the Puritans were not alienated from the word; on the contrary, they believed that the word had a potential revelation, linking humankind to the divine truth. For the Puritans, according to Ruland and Bradbury, "word and world alike were a shadowing forth of divine things, coherent systems of transcendent meanings" (19). It is from these transcendent meanings that post-revolutionary nineteenth century writers took some of their inspiration.

The Puritans wrote much, and read much too. They welcomed English books that were consistent with their conceptions, and some of these books were really read throughout the colony. And poetry, although limited by the religious situation, was an essential form of Puritan discourse. Some poems did achieve great success, such as Michael Wigglesworth's *The Day of Doom* (1662), a dramatic poem about the day of judgement, which was meant to instruct, to delight and to terrify.

Although the Puritans did not write novels, and

there is not a strong voice in imaginative prose fiction, Puritan culture did produce a kind of narrative that absorbed a high level of creative energy: the captivity narratives. Such narratives followed a pattern: a white settlement is attacked by "savages", most of the white people die, the survivors are taken prisoners, suffer all kind of humiliation, including being mutilated or killed; any survivors are then released for ransom. John Gyles's narrative of his years as a captive, first among the natives, afterwards among the French, not only describes the events of his captivity, but also the inner conflicts he suffers, for being raised as a puritan and having to deal with so many different kinds of heathen customs (Dorson 209-232). The narratives describe the events, but never forget the transcendent meaning, the idea that everything in their lives was ruled by divine providence, that they were like the Hebrews leaving Egypt looking for the Promised Land. The Puritans saw themselves as the chosen people in this Promised Land, the Native

Americans as the devil, and the narratives turn into allegories of salvation, not only for the narrator, but for the entire people. When describing the natives' customs, the captive never enters the depth of their tradition and culture, for it would not comply with the Puritan discourse. Such narratives, when published, were consciously shaped, with some parts added, others omitted, in order to convey the Puritan message. These captivity narratives certainly influenced nineteenth century writers like Cooper, Sedgwick and Child, whose texts make clear references to them. It is not possible to forget that two of the Pocahontas narratives from the colonial period, John Smith's and Ralph Hamor's, are the first captivity narratives in American Literature. Smith tells about his own abduction and also about Pocahontas's, while Hamor is the first one to describe the native girl as a captive.

John Smith's narrative, however, is different from the Puritans' narratives in many senses. First, he is not a

Puritan, and his writings have no other meaning to convey, but his own experiences in the wilderness. Nevertheless, his text establishes a pattern that is also used by the Puritan narratives when the captive is a man: he is not supposed to wait for ransom, and depends exclusively on himself and on the natives to survive. The great exception in John Smith's narrative is his rescue by a native girl, something that would not fit into the Puritan discourse. However, because she was afterwards Christianized, and married to a white man, the fact that she was not born a Christian is somehow overlooked.

1.2. FROM THE NON-PAREIL OF VIRGINIA TO A LONG SUFFERING ROMANTIC PRINCESS: THE PATH OF POCAHONTAS FROM A HISTORICAL CHARACTER TO A FICTIONAL HEROINE.

During her lifetime, Pocahontas had her story narrated by several writers, all assuring the reader they were narrating the true history of Virginia colonization. Among these writers, John Smith, William Strachey and Ralph Hamor are the most important ones, especially because they had really met her and witnessed some of her adventures. Their texts, John Smith's *A True Relation of Such Occurrences and Accidents of Noate as Hath Hapned in Virginia* ... (1608) and *The Generall Historie of Virginia, New England and the Summer Isles* ... (1624), the narratives that gave rise to the legends surrounding her name; William Strachey's *The Historie of Travaile Into Virginia Britannia* (1612), the only text that shows Pocahontas playing with the children in Jamestown; and Ralph Hamor's *A True Discourse of the Present State of*

Virginia (1615), the first to narrate her abduction and subsequent marriage to a white colonist, are still considered the basic texts for Pocahontas's biography. Two centuries later, when Americans remembered their nation's colonial history, Pocahontas was again celebrated for traveling to England as a Christianized Native American.

Many historians from the late seventeenth and the eighteenth century wrote about her as a historical character. None of them doubted John Smith's account, or imagined a love relationship between him and his savior. Robert Beverley, for instance, in *The History of Virginia* (1722), does not mention the rescue episode when narrating the first years of Virginia. When mentioning Pocahontas's marriage and her subsequent trip to England, he states that John Smith, in reaction to that event,

> used all the means he could to express his gratitude to her, as having formerly preserved his life by the hazard of her own; for, when by

the command of her father, Capt. Smith's head was upon the block to have his brains knocked out, she saved his head by laying hers close upon it (29)

Beverley then transcribed John Smith's 1616 "Letter to Queen Anne", published in 1624, the first text to mention the rescue. The historian does not discuss the veracity of the tale, but does not over value it either. At that moment, Pocahontas's conversion to the Christian faith and her marriage were the most discussed events in her life; through them, important Virginian families could claim to be descendants of the noble Native American princess. Aristocratic ascendance in Virginia was very important, and considering Pocahontas as a princess helped establish Virginia's own aristocracy. As Ann Uhry Abrams states, early in the eighteenth century "the plantation elite [in Virginia] were determined to substantiate the aristocratic credentials of Pocahontas" (64). Beverley's text, for instance, embellished the legend by stating that King James had not been happy about the

Emperor Powhatan's daughter's marriage to a commoner (33). And William Stith, in *The History of the First Discovery and Settlement of Virginia*, describes her as a British noblewoman who could speak good English, had good manners and was "well instructed in Christianity" (137).

Abrams also states that "[t]hese attempts to endow Pocahontas with a regal pedigree not only removed the heroine from hints of Indian 'savagery' but also turned attention away from the mixed blood that flowed through many elite Old Dominion veins" (64-65). Pocahontas's case was certainly an exception, for people of mixed blood were not usually well seen. As Tilton states, Pocahontas's noble descendants were "always distinguished from others of Indian-white descent during the colonial and early national periods" (11). He also argues that, during the colonial and early national periods, Pocahontas was remembered as a "flesh-and-blood Indian woman, who, as Europeans saw it, had turned her back on her people and her title. Pocahontas had converted, married an Englishman, and produced a son, and many of her descendants had become influential, highly visible members of southern society" (12).

The fact that Pocahontas was seen by the British as a princess, who had married a white man and had accepted Christian faith, together with the fact that her descendants had become important people in the colony, helped establish in Virginia an aristocracy of its own. Such an aristocracy was based on great plantations, which had their origin in the tobacco plantation of John Rolfe, and in the slave labor that began in Virginia in 1640 and was legally established in 1661.

In Beverley's text, there is no romanticizing; Pocahontas's relationship with John Smith is that of a friend, not of a lover. Their last meeting in Branford is narrated thus:

> Till this lady arrived in England, she had all along been informed that Captain Smith was dead, because he had been diverted from that

American Identity and the Myth of Pocahontas 81

> colony by making settlements in the second plantation, now called New England; for which reason, when she saw him, she seemed to think herself much affronted, for that they had dared to impose so gross an untruth upon her, and at first sight of him turned away. It cost him a great deal of intreaty, and some hours attendance, before she would do him the honor to speak to him; but at last she was reconciled, and talked freely to him. She put him in mind of her former kindnesses, and then upbraided him for his forgetfulness of her, showing by her reproaches, that even a state of nature teaches to abhor ingratitude. (32)

In no moment is there, in this narrative, the hint of a possible love relationship between the English adventurer and the Native American girl.

William Stith, in his 1747 text, which was used by later historians and biographers as a reliable source concerning the Virginia settlement, gives great emphasis to Pocahontas's marriage, which he describes as follows:

> Pocahontas was eagerly sought, and kindly entertained every where, Many Courtiers, and others of his Acquaintance, daily flocked to Captain Smith, to be introduced to her. They generally confessed, that the Hand of God did visibly appear, in her Conversion; and that they had seen many English Ladies, worse

Favoured, of less exact Proportion, and genteel Carriage, than she attented by the Lord, her Husband, and divers other Persons of Fashion and distinction. The whole Court were charmed and surprised, at the Decency and Grace of her Deportment; and the King himself, and Queen, were pleased, honourably to receive and esteem her. The Lady Delawarr, and those other Persons of Quality, also waited on her, to the Masks, Balls, Plays, and other public Entertainments. (Quoted in Mossiker, 255)

According to Mossiker, Stith's text may be based on family tradition, for his aunt, Anne Stith, was the second wife of Colonel Robert Bolling, whose first wife had been Pocahontas's granddaughter. Thus, Stith was "heir to family legend and tradition; he had heard stories told at first or second hand, from the lips of the Powhatan princess's direct descendants" (152). Possibly because of that or maybe due to his own will to be historical, his text is faithful to the sources he used, such as John Smith's and Ralph Hamor's texts. At no time does he suggest a love relationship between the Native American girl and the Captain. His emphasis on Pocahontas's sojourn in

England is clearly connected to the Virginian wish for an American aristocracy that had in Pocahontas its beginning and support.

After the American Revolution, there is a turning point in the narratives about the Native American maiden, who, at that time, was venerated both for her baptism into the Anglican Church and for saving the life of the English captain John Smith, who had emerged as an American hero shortly after the birth of the new republic. The very titles of the historical accounts demonstrate a different perspective. While Beverley and Stith wrote histories of Virginia, John Winthrop and Thomas Prince wrote histories of New England, other historians wrote about the other colonies; after the Revolution, when the thirteen colonies became the United States of America, a series of books about the History of the USA as a whole appeared, such as William Robertson's *The History of the Discovery and Settlement of America* (1796) and George Bancroft's *History of the United States* (1834). In these accounts,

Pocahontas's story acquires a different meaning. The rescue of John Smith becomes emblematic of the success of the colonization, for, in saving the captain's life, she supposedly saved the whole enterprise, since he was a very important figure in the white settlement. Her marriage becomes less important then, its importance shown to be local to Virginia, whose most prominent families claimed to be her descendants. John Smith's rescue, on the other hand, is important for the construction of the American nation as a whole, for, as colonial historian Thomas Wertenbaker says, "if there had been no Jamestown, there would have been no Plymouth" (Mossiker 4).

William Robertson, for instance, stresses the rescue episode:

> They led him, however, in triumph through various parts of the country, and conducted him at last to Powhatan, the most considerable Sachim in that part of Virginia. There the doom of death being pronounced he was led to the place of execution, and his head already bowed down to receive the fatal blow, when

> that fond attachment of the American women to their European invaders, the beneficial effects of which the Spaniards often experienced, interposed in his behalf. The favourite daughter of Powhatan rushed in between him and the executioner, and by her entreaties and tears prevailed on her father to spare his life. The beneficence of his deliverer, whom the early English writers dignify with the title of the Princess Pocahuntas, did not terminate here; she soon after procured his liberty, and sent from time to time seasonable presents of provisions (405-406).

The passage shows the interference of Pocahontas in a way that illustrates an European idea of Native American women. Although it does not imply a love relationship between the native girl and the British soldier, William Robertson shows it as a possibility. Six years later John Davis picks upon this possibility in one of his novels about Pocahontas, which tells of a true love story between her and the captain.

Before John Davis there is a pre-revolutionary narrative with a Pocahontas-like episode, in which her name is not mentioned: *The Female American* (1767), by

Unca Eliza Winkfield. The work is anonymous, for she used a pseudonym to publish the novel. According to Betty Joseph, in "Re (playing) Crusoe/Pocahontas", *The Female American* readdresses Crusoe's story through the narrative of Pocahontas. As she argues:

> because Robinson Crusoe became immensely popular at a time when the status of both the European woman and the colonial Other were being debated and inscribed into the discourses of the Enlightenment, it is very likely that the novel was easy game for a reader or writer interested in supplanting the white male of property as human norm (2)

Thus, there appears this anonymous novel that transforms "Defoe's castaway narrative into one of female self-fashioning and into a critique of colonialism at the same time" (2).

Like Daniel Defoe, who entitled his novel *The Life and Strange Adventures of Robinson Crusoe ... Written by Himself*, the author of the eighteenth century American novel named her book *The Female American, or The Extraordinary Adventures of Unca Eliza Winkfield,*

Compiled by Herself. However, she does not operate a simple transformation of Crusoe into a woman: in creating in her wake the figure of Pocahontas, she attempts to supersede her novelistic ancestors (Defoe and Crusoe), inaugurating a remarkably different civilizing project from that of her male counterparts. The Pocahontas moments in the novel are not only the rescue scene, but also the incidents where she serves as a mediator between her people and the strangers; this mediating function is also performed by Unca in Winkfield's novel. Yet, although the novel creates a fictional character with Pocahontas's features, it is not the first to give the Native American girl a fictional life: first, the author changed the heroine's name; second, the heroine was not indeed a Native American, but a mixed-blood girl. *The Female American* begins with a transatlantic journey by Unca's grandfather and father, Edward Winkfield and William Winkfield respectively, to join other British settlers in Virginia. Soon after their arrival, their plantation is attacked by Native Americans who take William Winkfield captive. In a reconstruction of the Pocahontas tale, the "king's" daughter Unca begs for his life; he is released and given to the "princess" in marriage. The couple is later permitted to leave the native village and go back to Winkfield's plantation, where their daughter (the protagonist-author, also named Unca) is born and raised in a way that mingled her Anglo and Native American heritage. This pre-revolutionary text already shows a transformation of the Pocahontas narrative, the inclusion of a love relationship between the native girl and the man she saves, that is to become more pronounced during the nineteenth century. Tilton and Mossiker also link Pocahontas to Unca, and suggest that it is a Pocahontas-like story, although both consider it a poor literary text. With John Davis, says William Warren Jenkins in "The Princess Pocahontas and three Englishmen named John", the presentation of the Pocahontas story assumed several new dimensions as he successfully adapted the legend in fiction and poetry" (13).

As White argues, history and fiction are easily intermingled. He states that historical narratives are "verbal fiction, the contents of which are as much invented as found" (82), thus having a strong connection with literature. This connection was even stronger at the beginning of the nineteenth century, when History was seen as a branch of literature. As Michael I. Carignan states in "Fiction as History or History as Fiction", "a long tradition views history as a branch or special form of literature, or an art-form" (5), and this happens till the middle of the nineteenth century. This may explain why writers like John Davis could so freely adapt a historical event into a literary one, while trying to narrate Virginia's history from a literary point of view.

Following up, I will discuss Romanticism, especially American Romanticism, which has its own characteristics. This discussion is important for different reasons: first of all, it will be very helpful for the understanding of the romantic literary texts under analysis in Chapter 3; second, it was under the influence of European Romanticism that John Davis produced his Pocahontas narratives, one of which is the basis for this dissertation; and third, it was during Romanticism that the modern concept of nation appears. Thus defining Romanticism and its features is crucial to the development of this work.

1.3. AMERICAN ROMANTICISM

For a better understanding of the importance of the Pocahontas narratives for the construction of an American national identity, it is necessary to remember that the post revolutionary period in the US was full of contradictions and conflicts. As Spiller points out, while on the one hand, the thirteen former colonies were conscious of their new situation as a new country, on the other hand, there were still many things to do before they could establish themselves before the world as a rightful nation (115). At the same time, American intellectuals were too close to European thought to just relinquish their ancestry. The Enlightenment, which was in its final years in Europe, had important American representatives, like Benjamin Franklin and Thomas Jefferson, two prominent figures of the American Revolution. As Maurice Cranston, in *The Romantic Movement*, states, "the United States was too much the creature of the Enlightenment, its culture too profoundly shaped by eighteenth-century nationalism and empiricism" (145), not being totally influenced by Romanticism, like the other countries in the Americas.

In many ways it is Benjamin Franklin who best represents the spirit of the Enlightenment in the USA: self-educated, social, confident, a man of the world, determined and public-spirited, speculative about the character of the world, but in matters of religion satisfied to observe the tangible conduct of men rather than to discuss mystic matters. Because of his enormous influence upon American thinkers, literary critics like Cranston argue that American national identity is not related to Romanticism as in other former colonies like Brazil, where the Romantic Movement appeared soon after independence. Because of the strong relationship between the Enlightenment and the beginning of American nationalism, Romantic texts only interfered in the construction of an American identity through non-canonical texts, texts that literary critics have considered as minor literary works (Cranston 145-147). But when literary critics and historians consider that Romanticism only appeared in the US around 1820, they do not take into consideration the popular drama with national themes or popular novels like *The Female American*, a clearly romantic text, or Davis's texts about American history and Pocahontas.

Romanticism, as an artistic and literary movement is closely related to the idea of nation. Maurice Cranston declares that the concept of 'nation' has always been a disputed one, and that nationalism has had a different form in different contexts. To him, these differences in turn "have had their effect not only on the ideals to which the romantic imagination has been directed, but on the tone and colour of romantic expression" (140). Although Cranston himself argues that Romanticism has not had such a role in the literary history of the USA, he points out that such a romantic influence may have happened through what he calls the "devious way" of popular literature, in which the plays about Pocahontas may be included.

According to Anthony Quinton, in "Romantic Irony", Romanticism must be seen as a "cluster of attitudes and preferences" that helps historians and literary critics to distinguish some writers from others. However, it is not definable "in a short formula made up of precisely demarcated terms" (778). Thus, it is easier to discuss some characteristics of such a complex phenomenon than to try giving it a concrete definition.

It is possible to say, then, that Romantic thinkers, still according to Quinton, favor "the concrete over the abstract, variety over uniformity, the infinite over the finite, nature over culture, convention and artifice, the organic over the mechanical, freedom over constraint, rules and limitations". Romantic writers also prefer, says Quinton, in human terms, "the unique individual to the average man, the free creative genius to the prudent man of good sense, the particular community or nation to humanity at large" (778).

In "The Influence of Philosophy", Quinton states that Romanticism was strongly dependent on philosophy. As he argues, Romantic emphasis on emotion and liberation comes from Rousseau, and the notion of a higher kind of reason comes from post-Kantian philosophers, like Fichte[5] and Schelling,[6] taken up most directly by the British Romantic writer Samuel Taylor Coleridge. Romantic affiliation, says Quinton, was Herder's idea of the unique individuality of particular peoples[7], which implies a nationalism that was affirmed by Fichte and bureaucratized by Hegel[8], also borrowed from Rousseau and Burke[9]. As Quinton says, "the way was prepared for the rampant nationalism of the nineteenth century and the erosion of dynastic absolutism" (673). This relationship between Romanticism and Philosophy certainly serves to reinforce the link between Romantic texts and the construction of national identities in the beginning of the nineteenth century, for it helps establish the very concept of nation, which acquires its modern meaning during Romanticism.[10]

Romanticism, as critics like Maurice Cranston and Jerome MacGann argue, is an intellectual and aesthetic phenomenon that emphasizes three main points. At fist, the Romantic universe is seen as a single unified whole, which means that everything is connected to everything else; second, the Romantic universe is seen as full of values, tendencies, and life; and third, the best way of perceiving reality, to the Romantic, is through some subjective feeling or intuition, which makes the poet participate in the subject of his/her own knowledge, instead of viewing it from the outside. However, due to the impossibility of giving a complete definition of Romanticism, it is crucial to the understanding of this movement in literature and the arts in general, to discuss some of its features, especially the ones that most differentiate Romanticism from previous schools of thought. The most important of these features, closely connected to the three points discussed above, is Individualism.

The cult of the individual was established by Jean Jacques Rousseau in his *Confessions* (1770; published in 1781), in which he also championed the freedom of the human spirit with his famous announcement "I felt before I thought" (19). As Thomas McFarland states in *Romanticism and the heritage of Rousseau*, the *Confessions* may be considered as the "inaugurating text of Romanticism", due to "the universality of its dissemination in the European reading public" and "its inexhaustible suggestive power" (51). McFarland also says that individualism and the emphasis on emotion over reason, stressed by Rousseau, influenced writers all over Europe. Such an influence can be seen in the German Romantic writer Johann Wolfgang von Goethe, whose play *Gotz von Berlichingen* (1773, translated into English in 1799) inaugurated the "Sturm und Drang" (storm and stress) movement, and whose novel *The Sorrows of Young*

Werther (1774, translated into English in 1779) set a tone and mood much copied by the Romantics in their works and often in their personal lives: a fashionable tendency to frenzy, melancholy, world-weariness, and even self-destruction. This emphasis on feelings was so strong that could justify a character committing suicide because of unrequited love.

In *Toward a Genealogy of Individualism*, Daniel Shanahan says that, as a literary and philosophical movement, Romanticism represents "what one might call a celebration of the empowered self". He also says that

> The individual -- fully conscious and anxious to test his or her powers of awareness to the utmost -- is the overriding Romantic motif, and the attitudes expressed by the Romantic artist are those of the empowered self: the self as the source of truth (in the case of the Romantics, truth as revealed through beauty) and the repository of spiritual meaning; the search for the self as the only avenue to true fulfillment; and -- tellingly -- the alienation of the self-aware individual, especially the artist, from the mass of humanity. (91)

As for American Romanticism, Individualism is

perhaps the primary concept that, transcending such categories as race, gender, class, age and region, unites Americans across time and space to give coherence to the national experience. From the earliest beginnings of the republic to the post-modernist present, the rights of the individual citizen and his or her place in the scheme of things have been of primary importance to American writers, philosophers, artists, political theorists, theologians and others concerned with articulating national values and principles. The development of the self became a major theme; self-awareness a primary method. If, according to Romantic theory, self and nature were one, self-awareness was not a selfish dead end but a mode of knowledge opening up the universe. If one's self were one with all humanity, then the individual had a moral duty to reform social inequalities and relieve human suffering. The idea of "self" — which suggested selfishness to earlier generations — was redefined. New compound words with positive meanings emerged: "self-realization," "self-expression," "self- reliance."

A very important movement, which is closely connected to American Romanticism, especially in what concerns individualism and the idealization of nature, is Transcendentalism. It is, like Romanticism, a movement that defies neat definition. The main principles of Transcendentalism were established by Ralph Waldo Emerson in his book *Nature* (1836), considered by Harmon Smith, in *My Friend, My Friend: The Story of Thoreau's Relationship with Emerson*, as "one of the great manifestos of American Transcendentalism" (72). These principles are: 1) all objects are miniature versions of the universe; 2) intuition and conscience "transcend" experience and reason; 3) man is one with nature; and 4) God is everywhere, in nature and in man (Bayn *et al* 384-412). Seen as an extension of Romanticism by most of the critics, Transcendentalism was its philosophical aspect, focusing primarily upon intuition and emotion over reason, and idealizing nature as an important part of human life, man himself being a part of it. It is through this philosophy that romantic individualism becomes stronger and fully justified in the US.

In aesthetic terms, romantic individualism was constituted by the uprising of feeling against forms — the rejection of classical equilibrium in favor of Romantic asymmetry. Embracing the unknown, and unafraid of the oppositions of human life, Romanticism overthrew the philosophic, artistic — even geographical — limitations of the Enlightenment. The ideal Romantic figure was the Wanderer, literally and figuratively voyaging in search of new lands, new places in the imagination, and new views for the soul. This figure, as Robert Spillman and Deborah Stein state in *Poetry into Song: Performances and Analysis of Lieder*, represents the "Heightened Individuality" of Romantic writings in their need "to explore the unknown and the dichotomous" (6)

As Romanticism developed everywhere, imagination was praised over reason, emotions over logic, and intuition over science — paving the way for a vast body of literature of great sensibility and passion. Literature from this period emphasized a new flexibility of form adapted to varying context and fast moving plots, and allowed mixed genres (the tragicomedy, the mingling of the grotesque and the sublime, and the melodrama) and freer style. Certain themes were, nevertheless, present in almost all nineteenth century writers, either European or American:

First: A sense of liberty, due to the Romantic philosophy itself, in which the desire to be free from convention and tyranny, as well as a strong emphasis on the rights and dignity of the individual were established. According to critics like Cranston and McGann, many of the libertarian and abolitionist movements of the late eighteenth and early nineteenth centuries were stimulated by this philosophy. In the same way the insistence on rational, formal, and conventional subject matter that had typified neoclassicism was reversed, many authoritarian regimes that had stimulated and supported neoclassicism in the arts were subjected to popular revolutions. Political and social causes became dominant themes in Romantic poetry and prose throughout the Western world. There was a general Romantic dissatisfaction with the organization of society that was often transcribed into specific criticism of urban society. Earlier, Rousseau had written that people were born free but that everywhere civilization put them in chains (*Social Contract* 3). This feeling of oppression was frequently expressed in poetry, fiction and drama, and served as philosophical support to the American and French Revolutions.

Second: The valorization of nature, with a delight in unspoiled scenery and in the (presumably) innocent life of rural dwellers. Often combined with this feeling for rural life is a generalized romantic melancholy, a sense that change is eminent and that a way of life is being threatened. For the romantic, Nature was, indeed, a constant companion and teacher — both benevolent and cruel. It became the arena in which the human drama was performed, the context in which a human being came to understand his/her place in the universe. Throughout Romantic literature, music and art, Nature is a vibrant presence, a character who speaks in a language of symbols at once mysterious and anthropomorphic, who keeps man in a dialogue with the life-force, itself. The idealization of nature is associated with, Steven Kreis argues in "Toward a Definition of Romanticism", the belief "in the natural goodness of man, the idea that man in a state of nature would behave well but is hindered by." He also states that "[t]he 'savage' is noble, childhood is good and the emotions inspired by both beliefs causes the heart to soar", while "urban life and the commitment to 'getting and spending,' generate a fear and distrust of the world." Thus, if man is "inherently sinful, reason must restrain his passions, but if he is naturally good, then in an appropriate environment, his emotions can be trusted" (4). The Romantic philosophies of Rousseau affected the popular understanding in such a way as to make Americans believe in the essential goodness and nobility to be found in unspoiled nature. As MacDonald says. "[w]hen the Indian was not a devil, he might be thought a noble savage" (7). However, it was not Rousseau who coined the expression "noble savage". It was created by the English poet John Dryden in 1672 in his play *Conquest of Granada*, in the voice of his character Almanzor, a Native American who grew up alone in the state of nature:

> But know that I alone am king of me.
> I am as free as Nature first made man,
> Ere the base laws of servitude began,
> When wild in woods the *noble savage* ran.
> (David Nichol Smith 29)

This connection between Native Americans and nature is perceived in several texts about Pocahontas, in which this relationship is presented positively, nature representing lack of corruption, purity. Such an aspect is discussed in Chapter 3, during the analysis of some Romantic texts on Pocahontas.

The idea of the savage as noble is just one side of the coin. Adriana Rissetto, in "Romancing the Indian: Sentimentalizing and Demonizing In Cooper and Twain", states that the natives were either portrayed as villain or as "naturalistic saints" (3). To her, "[t]hese polarities, demonizing and idealizing, are different forms of romanticizing: idealization romanticizes the positive, and demonization romanticizes the negative." She argues that "[b]oth terms are expressions of extravagance: the former is extravagant praise, and the latter is extravagant criticism. Neither courts reality more than the other; both equally ignore it" (3).

Third: A lure of the exotic, in which there is an expansion of the writers' imaginary horizons both spatially and chronologically. The shapeless world of dreams, the dark terrors of the mind as well as the confusing heights of creativity and the stunning beauties of nature in exotic lands — these were all way stations along the Romantic hero's path. As Renata Wasserman argues, European writers Europeanized the exotic and then made it available for American use, which means that, after independence, American writers started to use the exotic as a way to establish a national identity, as in the narratives of Cooper. Slotkin's point of view is similar to Wasserman's in relation to the different use European and American writers have made of the Native American. As he points out: "It was inevitable that the movement of the American literary mind during the Romantic era should be, figuratively and to a degree literally, a movement towards the Indian" (371). The Pocahontas story, which was, in a first moment, a European narrative concerning the New World, after the American Revolution, and especially during Romanticism, was incorporated into a new literature, particularly in popular dramas and poems, which makes it possible to set up a parallel between these narratives and the nation's founding narratives of Cooper.

Romanticizing Pocahontas, as John Davis first did,

includes her figure in the Noble Savage versus Bad Savage dichotomy, in which she represents the noble, good, sanctified Indian for her actions towards the white settlers, while her relatives, sometimes her father, sometimes her uncle, represent the ignoble, bad, demonized Indian for their acts against the Englishmen. Throughout this dissertation, this is a point of discussion when comparing the Pocahontas narratives to the other romantic tales.

Romanticism, together with its transcendental philosophy, can be connected to the creation of a popular literary tradition in the U.S. This happens because Romanticism, as well as Transcendentalism, champions individual freedom and personal liberty so appreciated by authors of popular novels. While political texts of the beginning of the nineteenth century were still more connected to the ideas of the Enlightenment, like the writings of Thomas Jefferson (*Letters*, 1789-1826) and John Taylor (*An Examination of the Late Proceedings in*

Congress, respecting the Official Conduct of the Secretary of the Treasury, 1793), some popular texts were already romantic, especially some novels, like the texts of James Fenimore Cooper (*Precaution*, 1820), Washington Irving ("The Devil and Tom Walker", 1800); some poems, like Joel Barlow's *The Columbiad* (1807), and, especially, the popular drama with national themes. When Romanticism finally enters within the canonical literature, as in Nathaniel Hawthorne's texts and through the influence of Transcendentalism, American readers were already used to reading romantic popular texts, including the popular dramas and poems about Pocahontas.

The next section of this chapter deals with the moment right after the American Revolution, when US writers were trying to ascertain their own identity and their own history. The Revolution itself brought a strong sense of nationalism, and the writers felt an enormous need to inscribe themselves in the history of the new nation they were helping to build. An important event, another war, strengthened this sense of nationalism and brought a new way of dealing with the Native Americans that strongly influenced the literature of the period.

1.4. From British Colony to Independent Nation: The Post-Revolutionary Period in the United States of America

Right after the American Revolution an internal war began: a struggle to establish where lies, indeed, the origin of the American nation, if in Jamestown or in Plymouth. Such an intellectual debate intended to establish not the historical beginning, once it was easy to prove that the Virginia colonization started earlier. The debate was to decide which of the settlements was really important for the construction of an American identity. The discussion occurs because, by the end of the eighteenth century, the Puritans were beginning to be acknowledged as the group that had "laid the moral and intellectual groundwork for the Revolution" (Tilton 37)[11]. Virginia, however, was the first successful English settlement in the US, and many important Virginians took part in the independence process as leaders of the Revolution, including George Washington and Thomas

Jefferson, first and third presidents of the new republic. Thus, a series of texts from this time, arguing for the primacy of Virginia, foreground Jamestown and the Pocahontas episode. Chief Justice John Marshall, in *The Life of George Washington*, includes not only events from the life of Washington, but also a description of the proceedings that foreshadowed Washington's appearance in the world stage. He justifies the inclusion stating that:

> [T]he history of general Washington, during his military command and civil administration, is so much that of his country, that the work appeared to the author to be most sensibly incomplete and unsatisfactory, while unaccompanied by such a narrative of the principal events preceding our revolutionary war, as would make the reader acquainted with the genius, character, and resources of the people about to engage in that memorable contest. (xvi)

Of these "principal events", three concerned Pocahontas's life: John Smith's rescue, her abduction and her marriage. When describing the rescue scene, Marshall explains Pocahontas's attitude in saving John Smith as "that enthusiastic and impassioned humanity which, in every climate, and in every state of society, finds its home in the female bosom" (28). Although he is not specific about the kind of feeling this humanity provoked in Pocahontas, Marshall, just like William Robertson years before, hints at the possibility of a love relationship between Pocahontas and John Smith that is well used by Davis. Though pre-romantic in chronological terms, Davis's texts are certainly romantic in the way they present the native girl and the events that surrounded her life. As Tilton suggests, "Davis can now be seen as having produced a precocious expression of what would come to be known as American Romanticism" (35).

The post-revolutionary period is marked by a growing sense of nationalism and by different ways of dealing with the Native Americans, who were by then seen as a threat to the development of the American nation. In 1812 these feelings toward the natives changed due to the war against England, a war that some historians like John K. Mahon, in *The War of 1812*, calls "the second war of independence" (31). Some Native Americans allied themselves with the British and, by the end of the war, they were no longer seen as threats. In 1812, the American War of Independence was still in the living memories of British and American peoples and governments. England still suffered the pain of losing a prized colony, while the US was eager to make itself more secure from foreign interference. Consequently, it did not take long to get the blood of both countries up, and a conflict of wills, at least, was a certainty.

According to Donald R. Hickey, in *The War of 1812: a Forgotten Conflict*, the war of 1812 is one of the less remembered US wars. It lasted for over two years, and ended much as it had started: in stalemate. Yet, it was a war that finally and forever confirmed American independence. As Scheckel states,

> [h]aving tested its strength against other world powers in the War of 1812, the new nation became self-consciously concerned with constructing an idea of 'America' that could reach beyond the founding act of revolution to

offer post-revolutionary generations a source of national identity and legitimacy (7).

At its close, Americans turned their energies to exploring and settling the American continent in a fury of westward expansion, for the war caused a clear decline of US dependence on European powers, and stimulated a sense of nationality that was to become stronger as new states were formed and new lands annexed to the country (Scheckel 7)

Scheckel also suggests that the war of 1812 marked a turning point in US attitudes toward Native Americans. With peace finally settled between the US and Britain, and as Americans laid claim to practically all land east of the Mississippi, it was difficult for them to imagine Native Americans uniting again to become a serious military or political threat. Henry Clay, in some comments as a Speaker of the House, in 1819, expresses this shift in attitude. At the beginning of the colonies' establishment, Clay noted, "we were weak ... [the Native Americans] were comparatively strong, ... they were the lords of the soil, and we were seeking ... asylum among them" (640). Now, however, things had changed:

> We are powerful and they are weak ... ['T]o use a figure drawn from their own sublime eloquence, the poor children of the forest have been driven by the great wave which has flowed in from the Atlantic ocean to almost the base of the Rocky Mountains, and, overwhelming them in its terrible progress, has left no other remains of hundreds of tribes, now extinct, than those which indicate the remote existence of their former companion, the mammoth of the New World. (640)

A combination of sorrow and triumph can be noted on Clay's choice of words, a common attitude toward the Native Americans at the beginning of the nineteenth century, as Brian Dippie suggests in *The Vanishing American*. Indeed, from the war of Independence through the middle of the nineteenth century, the idea that Native Americans were doomed to disappear was so widespread that Dippie called it a national "habit of thought" (15). Terrible as the Native Americans' fate might be, Clay's language certainly makes it sound inevitable. Turned from "lords of the soil" to "poor children of the forest", the only threat they could pose to the US was some moral discomfort. The views about the Native Americans in reality soon influenced the way literature deals with their figure, although there is a contradictory view of the natives by this period: while in real life they were subjected to the white government and were not seen as American citizens, but as objects to the white society's wish, in literature they were portrayed in two different ways, as nobles or as devils, but never as weak and submissive.

In the novels of Cooper and in popular dramas with native themes, the natives were either idealized or demonized. It is in this aspect that American Romanticism most differs from British Romanticism: romantic writers as a whole were not satisfied with their own time and, in order to evade it, wrote about the distant past or distant lands. In Europe, the Middle Ages became a preferred setting for romantic adventure, as well as the Orient and the Americas, for being exotic in European terms. In the US, writers like Cooper and Longfellow did not want to look at the European past as their own. Instead, they looked at an American past itself. Three ways of dealing with such a past, then, appeared: either the writer saw the natives' past as part of the American past and history, or he totally denied it, considering American history as if beginning only from the moment of the European arrival, or, as a third alternative, they saw a close connection between the natives' past and their own through the presence of a mediator figure, usually a female native. It is in such a context that Pocahontas's story appears as a true romantic love story.

Aspects such as national identity and nationalism, liminal figures and power relationship between colonizer and colonized can be better explained through the theories that underlie this dissertation. Such theories are developed in the following chapter.

2

EXPLAINING THEORIES: CRUCIAL VIEWS OF NATION AND NATIONAL IDENTITY, MISCEGENATION, LIMINAL FIGURES AND CAPTIVITY NARRATIVES

> *Nations, like narrative, lose their origins in the myths of time and only fully realize their horizons in the mind's eye*
>
> Homi K. Bhabha [1]
>
> *Race is a text (an array of discursive practices), not an essence. It must be read with painstaking care and suspicion, not imbibed.*
>
> Henry Louis Gates Jr [2]
>
> *To survive in the Borderlands*
> *You must live sin fronteras*
> *Be a crossroads*
>
> Gloria Anzaldúa [3]

> *Oh, the roaring and singing and dancing and yelling of those black creatures in the night, which made the place a lively resemblance of hell.*
>
> Mrs. Mary Rowlandson [4]

This chapter discusses several concepts necessary to an understanding of how the romantic texts on Pocahontas and the texts of James Fenimore Cooper, Catherine Maria Sedgwick and Lydia Maria Child, in dealing with racial issues, liminal figures and captivities narratives, helped establish an American national identity. Although some of these concepts, such as national identity and miscegenation, may seem to be disconnected, throughout this chapter I try to demonstrate how they, as well as concepts like liminal figures and captivity among different peoples, are closely related to the construction of an American national identity.

2.1. NATION AND NATIONAL IDENTITY

Since this dissertation is focused on an attempt to connect the Pocahontas narratives to those of James Fenimore Cooper as founding narratives of the American nation, the concepts of nation and national identity must be established. Such concepts, in this dissertation, are based on the theories of Ernest Renan, Benedict Anderson, and Homi Bhabha. Renan, in "What is a Nation?", one of the earliest and most significant reflections on the meaning of nationhood, suggests that "the essence of a nation is that all individuals have many things in common, and also that they have forgotten many things" (11). According to Renan, the nation depends on acts of remembering and forgetting, which means that the violence that may have helped to build a nation must be forgotten so that it can be reimagined as a "family" history — the history of the nation (19). Recent theorists of nation and nationalism, such as Benedict Anderson and

Homi Bhabha[5], have argued that Renan's moment of forgetting may be the actual beginning of a nation. For Anderson, in *Imagined Communities*, the nation begins like a realistic novel, "with its spectacular possibilities for the representation of simultaneous actions in homogeneous empty time" (194), in which "a sociological organism moving calendrically through [it] is a precise analogue of the idea of the nation, which is also conceived as a solid community moving steadily through history" (26). Two events happening simultaneously, though in different places, can connect the people involved in those happenings by the accurate "simultaneity", that is, they share an awareness of a collective temporal dimension in which they co-exist. For Bhabha, in *The Location of Culture*, the nation emerges in a liminal space that reveals "the ambivalence of the 'nation' as a narrative strategy" (140). Whether in one way or the other, the idea of the nation begins in a moment of forgetting that is motivated by a desire to remember in order to work out the gap between individual and collectivity, to fill the space between "immemorial past" and "limitless future", as Anderson argues (11-12) or to narrate in "that strange time — forgetting to remember" — the "liminality of cultural modernity itself", as suggested by Bhabha (161, 140).

Anderson proposes a definition of nation as "an imagined political community" (6). Imagined because no mater how small the nation is, none of the individual members will ever meet or know all of the others. Therefore, the existence of some form of communion between particular groups of people must be imagined. A nation is a community because, no matter what are the actual inequalities that might exist within the nation, it is at base "conceived as a deep, horizontal comradeship" (7). One of the ways in which a nation is imagined for its citizens is through narrative, through the narration of particular events and their deployment within an overall biography of the nation. In this biography, it is important for the imaginative construction of the nation to have historically distant origins, either actual or invented: "If nation-states are widely conceded to be the 'new' and 'historical', the nations to which they give political expression always loom out of the immemorial past and, still more important, glide into the limitless future" (Anderson 11).

In *The Invention of Tradition*, Eric Hobsbawn argues that an invented tradition "is taken to mean a set of practices, ... which seek to inculcate certain values and norms of behaviour by repetition, which automatically implies continuity with the past". As he explains, "they [rules and norms] normally attempt to establish [a] continuity with a suitable historic past" (1), the immemorial past so necessary to the construction of a national identity. In relation to the creation of a U.S. national identity, the appropriation or even "invention" of Native American identity either by figures or within the discourses concerned with the US nation building is, as

Stephen Germic argues, in "Border Crossing and the Nation: The Natural History of Nativ(ist) American Identity", "utterly inseparable from the violent appropriation of territory held by native peoples." This way, "[t]he consequent development of the idea of 'nation' among indigenous peoples in the United States is likewise inseparable from ongoing struggles to regain illegally expropriated land" (2).

Anthony D. Smith, in *Myths and Memories of the Nation*, states that there are two distinct positions for the studying of the concepts of nation and nationalism: the "primordialists", who believe in the historical longevity of nationalism and ethnicity; and the "modernists", who have pronounced the nation an essentially modern creation, with few roots in pre-modern times. Although he considers himself a primordialist, while Anderson is clearly a modernist, his concept of nation seems to give a basis for Anderson's concept: "[A nation] is a named human population sharing an historic territory, common myths and historical memories, a mass public culture, a common economy and common legal rights and duties for all members" (14). Although the 'communities' may in a sense be imagined, as Anderson declares, the states around which they coalesce are all too real.

To Bhabha, the narrative of the nation is intrinsically unstable. His view most generally indicates a people, a nation, or a national culture as "an empirical sociological category or a holistic cultural entity". Therefore, "the narrative and psychological force that nationess brings to bear on cultural production and political projection is the effect of the ambivalence of the 'nation' as a narrative strategy" (*Location of Culture* 140). For the purpose of this dissertation, nation will be seen according to the modernists' concepts, although having in mind that both the ideas of the primordialists and modernists can be used to clarify some important aspects when discussing the construction of an American national identity.

American Identity and the Myth of Pocahontas

Narrating a nation does not mean, necessarily, establishing a national cultural identity, but it is certainly an important part of this process. Such an identity, however, is not a fixed and determined thing. As Stuart Hall says, in *A Identidade Cultural na Pós-Modernidade*, "national identities are not things we are born with, but are formed and transformed inside the *representation*" (48 – emphasis on the original)[6]. Thus, a national cultural identity can be multiple and changeable according to specific historical moments. As Hall argues, in "Cultural Identity and Diaspora", "[c]ultural identities are the points of identification, the unstable points of identification or suture, which are made, within the discourses of history and culture. Not an essence, but a *positioning*" (113 – emphasis on the original). Thus, having in mind the impossibility of a definite or stable national identity, this dissertation wants to highlight the possibility of an American identity, which was constructed with the help of the Pocahontas narratives after the American Revolution.

Wars of national independence undoubtedly lead citizens from a certain nation to imagine and construct the nation through different narratives. This process of narrativization takes place when an ex-colony becomes a new nation. In the United States of America, the American Revolution, which settled their independence, happened right before Romanticism arrived in America. Although some authors, such as Karl Beckson and Thomas Hampson, state that Romanticism, as a literary movement, only came to America in the 1820's, pre-romantic texts, like Philip Freneau's "The Indian Burying Ground" (1787) and Joel Barlow's *The Columbiad* (1807), were already published and read, some of them trying to foreground a different narrative in order to establish an American national identity. Some of the narratives about Pocahontas, like John Davis's *Travels of Four Years and a Half in the United States of America*, are inserted in this context.

Franz Fanon, in *The Wretched of the Earth*, defines

culture as the "first expression of a nation, the expression of its preferences of its taboos and its patterns" (244). A national culture would, then, be defined as the "sum total of all these appraisal; it is the result of internal and external tensions exerted over society as a whole and also at every level of that society" (244). The condition for the existence of a national culture is the very existence of a nation. As Fanon argues:

> The nation is not only the condition of culture, its fruitfulness, its continuous renewal, and its deepening. It is also a necessity. It is the fight for national existence which sets culture moving and opens to it the doors of creation. Later on it is the nation which will ensure the conditions and framework necessary to culture. The nation gathers together the various indispensable elements necessary for the creation of a culture, those elements which alone can give it credibility, validity, life and creative power. In the same way it is its national character that will make such a culture open to other cultures and which will enable it to influence and permeate other cultures. A non-existent culture can hardly be expected to have bearing on reality, or to influence reality. The first necessity is the re-establishment of the nation in order to give life to national culture in the strictly biological sense of the phrase (244-45)

Fanon is here referring to former African colonies in their need to (re-)establish themselves as nations, but his concept can be also applied to the construction of new nations such as in the case of the US, whose beginning is characterized by having the quest for a national cultural identity within the circulation of literary texts, documents, journals, newspapers, etc. Within this context, the Native Americans' culture becomes, then, a problem, for, although not belonging to the American idealized nation that had given them a place in the "immemorial past" without an active role in their present society, they were living persons who wished to be heard. As Germic argues, early natural scientists, studying American 'pre'-history "appropriated an idealized or even fantasized Native American identity to elaborate a national culture and a universal while exclusive identity that served to justify the territorial appropriation of continental expansion" (8), displacing the natives in reality while idealizing them in fictional texts.

In ex-colonies, the concept of nation is sometimes related to the mixing of the different people that have helped in its formation. In relation to the US, this concern is quite important: in forgetting the violence that generated the nation, Americans have to forget the violence Anglo American people have imposed upon Native American and vice-versa, avoiding mention of the inevitable ethnic mixtures that happened during the building of the nation. Next, there is a discussion about these mixtures and their influence on the building of an American national identity.

2.2. MISCEGENATION

The word "miscegenation" did not exist before 1863, when David Goodman Croly coined it in an eponymous pamphlet, *Miscegenation: the Theory of the Blending of the Races, Applied to the American White Man and Negro*. According to Tilton, this word, which is now regarded as a "biased expression reflecting racial prejudice and the assumption that intermarriage is unnatural and wrong" (189), was at first intended to have a positive meaning. Croly justifies his reasons to have coined the word and all of its related forms:

> *Reasons for coining these words.* – (1.)There is, as yet, no word in the language which expresses exactly the idea they embody. (2.) Amalgamation is a poor word, since it properly refers to the union of metals with quicksilver, and was, in fact, only borrowed for an emergency, and should now be returned to its proper signification. (3.) The words used above are just the ones wanted, for they express the ideas with which we are dealing, and, what is quite important, they express nothing else. (vii)

He also states that "[t]he word is spoken at last. It is

Miscegenation – the blending of the various races of men — the practical recognition of the brotherhood of all of the children of the common father" (v). Croly makes clear that he favors the mixing of races, be this mix between the white and black races or between the white and the Native Americans.

Although the word itself was not in use during the historical period I am dealing with, theories and laws against the mixing of different races already existed. As early as 1662, Virginia had a law forbidding interracial marriage, with an amendment in 1691 that removed any doubt whether or not Native Americans should be included in this ban:

> . . . For prevention of that abominable mixture and spurious issue which hereafter may increase in this dominion, as well as by negroes, mulattos, and Indians intermarrying with English, or other white women, as by their unlawfull accompanying with one another, Be it enacted . . . that . . . whatsoever English or other white man or woman being free, shall intermarry with a negro, mulatto or Indian man or woman bond or free shall within three months after such marriage be

> banished and removed from this dominion forever.... (Act XVI)

In New England, a 1786 law specifically banned intermarriage between natives and whites. Other states also had such statutes, and in all cases it was made clear to whites that for their own good, and the good of their states, they should not marry non-white partners.

Discussing these issues is important to understand why Pocahontas's story is seen as an exception, and also why, in some of the Pocahontas narratives her marriage to John Rolfe is not mentioned. If such a marriage was not forbidden when it actually happened, it would have been clearly an illegal act during the period of the publication of such narratives.

These laws, however, were not the only reason to keep the races apart. David H. Fowler in *Northern Attitudes toward Interracial Marriage* summarizes some of the other obstacles an interracial couple had to overcome before they could be together:

> There were, in addition to striking differences in physical appearance, great cultural disparities between the two races. The Indians spoke languages strange to Europeans, had neither a technology advanced beyond the Stone Age nor a literature, depended on hunting and fishing more than crop cultivation for subsistence, and often appeared to the colonists as unpredictable, treacherous, cruel and dirty. The fact that the aborigines were also pagans was a cultural difference of great importance to the Christian newcomers. (26)

Such "cultural disparities", clearly outlined in numerous popular captivity narratives, with strong stress on the apparent savagery of the natives, and certainly the Christians' additional fear of this sort of mixing that would be sinful no matter the circumstances, were enough for the white settlers to stay away from marrying the natives. Another reason to avoid intermarriage, and indeed all sexual intercourse between the races, was the thought of the children that might be produced by such a union, who were seen as not belonging anywhere.

Although Native Americans were considered as "primitive" or "noble savage" since the beginning of colonization, it is during the eighteenth century that the idea of primitiveness achieves greater popularity. As Lilia Moritz Schwarcz states, in *O Espetáculo das Raças*, they were seen as primitive because they were the first, the "original", in the beginning of human species. Native Americans became, then, "privileged objects to a new perception that reduced humankind to one species, a single evolution and a possible perfectibility"[7] (44). A key concept in Rousseau's humanistic theory, "perfectibility" resumed — together with the freedom of resisting or accepting nature's demands — a very human specificity. Different from the conception to be used by evolutionists during the nineteenth century, the humanist vision stated that all human beings had the capacity to improve themselves. Mark of a single humanity, but with different ways, "human perfectibility" announced to Rousseau the "vices" of civilization, the origin of inequality among men. After all, all human beings are born equal, just without a complete definition from nature (Rousseau 209).

Evolutionists, like the Comte de Buffon and Lamarck, believed in the differences among different races, privileging the white race above the others and stating that only whites could really improve themselves. Such evolutionists had two opposing views, both considering European white people as superior to any other people. These opposing views concerned the origin of humankind, which appeared in philosophical texts long before Darwin and the concepts of human evolution. On the one hand, there is the idea of "Monogenism", which says that all human being has the same origin, as it is established in the Bible. It is accepted by the Christian churches and by most thinkers before nineteenth century either in Europe or in the Americas. Monogenism, then, is based upon the conception that humankind originated from Adam and Eve, a single source. All other differences among races arose as an effect of degeneration of humans since creation. On the other side, there is the idea of "Polygenism", which establishes that each human "race" has a different origin. This hypothesis was first described by the French writer Isaac de la Peyrére, in the mid seventeenth century in a book that was burned in Paris, possibly because of, as Rachel Caspari and Milford Wolpoff state, in *Race and Human Evolution*, "its claim that of all humankind, only the Jews descended from the creation represented by Adam and Eve" (59), while all others come from pre-Adamite creations. However, Polygenism was first clearly expressed in the latter eighteenth century by the Scottish philosopher Henry Home, Lord Kames, who proposed the idea in *Sketches of the History of Man*, in 1774. Noting what he considered to be a great number of human variations, he suggested that God had

> created many pairs of the human race, differencing from each other both externally and internally; that he fitted those pairs for different climates and placed each pair in its proper climate, and that the peculiarities of the original pairs were preserved entire in their descendants (Caspari and Wolpoff 60).

In spite of being rejected by most scientists and

philosophers, polygenism was well established in the US, especially during the nineteenth century, after the American Revolution, when American writers and thinkers were narrating their new nation. If it could be proved that Native Americans and Blacks were different species, then they should not be included in the declaration that "all men are created equal".[8]

According to Thomas F. Gossett, in *Race: The History of an Idea in America*, it was Charles White, a Manchester physician, who argued in 1799 in his "An Account of the Regular Gradation in Man", that Africans, Asians, Europeans and Native Americans were separate species. He classified "Negroes" as closer to apes than to Europeans, and appealed to the medieval concept of the Chain of Being[9] to justify the assumption of Black inferiority (47). Polygenesis was thus the indication of nineteenth century racism and as a justification for slavery and colonization.

Gossett also states that a Philadelphia scientist

Samuel Morton compared the physiological appearance of Africans with that of whites and Asians and derived a hierarchy of status and ability. Cranial capacities were measured and indexed by Dr. Morton, and cultures and civilizations were compared with climactic conditions. Morton collected crania from all over the world, assuming that the size of the cranium was synonymous with intelligence. He "concluded" that Negroes had the smallest cranial capacity, Native Americans were next, while Caucasians possessed the largest cranial capacity (58-61). Writing in the 1830s and 1840s, Morton's "scientific" study justified and supported the practice of slavery in the United States.

For Rousseau, however, with the notion of the "natural man", the idea of men overcoming themselves to achieve perfectibility is absolutely present. However, there were negative interpretations of his theories. In 1758, Swedish botanist Carolus Linnaeus established the classification system still in use for various forms of life.

He listed four categories that he labeled as "varieties" of the human species. To each he attributed inherited biological as well as learned cultural characteristics. He described *Homo Europæus* as light-skinned, blond, and governed by laws; *Homo Americanus* was copper-colored and was regulated by customs; *Homo Asiaticus* was sooty and dark-eyed and governed by opinions; *Homo Afer* was black and indolent and governed by impulse. It is possible, in retrospect, to recognize the ethnocentric assumptions involved in these descriptions, which imply a descending order of prestige. Most striking is the labeling of the four varieties as governed by laws, customs, opinions, and impulse, with Europeans on the top and Africans at the bottom. Thus, as the Native Americans were seen as racially inferior, they were not uncorrupted like Rousseau's natural man. Instead, they began to be considered as inherently evil. Several thinkers contributed to this more negative vision of America but two of them certainly deserve more attention: the Comte de Buffon, with his 1749 thesis of "American childishness", and Corneille de Pauw, with his theory of "American degeneration".

Long before the arising of racial theories, the first British settlers in America already had the notion of the Native Americans either as "childish" or as "evil" beings, depending on the way they (the natives) behaved in their first contact with the Europeans. In Virginia, for instance, because the Algonquians very well received the English people, the idea of the natives as "childish" is more or less accepted till 1622, when the massacre of Jamestown occurred. Then, their image as "evil doers" became stronger. In New England, from the very beginning it was the notion of the natives as a "degenerate race" that prevailed.

Thomas Jefferson, in *Notes on the State of Virginia*, rejects Buffon's theories, even writing to the French scientist to refute his claim that human and animal life in America was degenerative and therefore inferior to the life forms in Europe. Buffon believed, Jefferson wrote, "that nature is less active, less energetic on one side of the globe than she is on the other" (169), and added, with more than a hint of sarcasm, "as if both sides were not warmed by the same genial sun" (169), then launched into a lengthy refutation of Buffon's hypothesis with convincing evidence that animals are actually larger in America than in Europe. As Merril D. Peterson states, in *Thomas Jefferson and the New Nation*, the mastodon, or mammoth, was Jefferson's clincher; Europe had produced no animal to match this behemoth. His shipment of mastodon fossils to Paris, therefore, was not entirely Enlightenment altruism; it was also a final salvo in a scientific war. Buffon's suggestion that infant America was nature's retardate drove him to collect the ancient bones of the mammoth. When he received his fossils, he catalogued them carefully and precisely, as was his habit, sending them off to Philadelphia for admiration and to Paris for edification. He kept a few choice specimens, however, for his Monticello museum — trophies of a sort in commemoration of his private victory in the battle of New World versus Old (254-256). From this "battle" on, it is possible to perceive the beginning of a "general science of man" marked by the tension between a negative image of American nature and Native Americans, and the positive representation of the natural status presented by Rousseau. On one side, there is the humanist view, heir of the French Revolution, which naturalized human equality; on the other side, a still incipient reflection about the basic differences that exist among human beings. As Schwarcz argues, by the beginning of the nineteenth century, the second position gains force, establishing rigid correlations between genetic patrimony, intellectual capacity and moral inclinations (47).

In fact, the term "race" is used for the first time in a more specialized literature by Georges Cuvier, in *Research on the Fossil Bones of Quadrupeds* (1812), introducing the idea of the existence of permanent physical inheritance between the several human groups. Racial discourse was, thus, officially established by scientists, and its influence on literature was enormous. If before such theories were published there were already texts that were against interracial marriages, after them banning of interracial marriages became much more frequent, especially due to the theories that considered miscegenation as the greatest danger to the white people, since the mixed people would always inherit the negative features of both "races", representing then degeneration. Avoiding miscegenation was a way to maintain the superiority of the white race over the others.

Thus, as Adriana Rissetto points out, representations of Native Americans, in the late eighteenth century and throughout the nineteenth century, were seldom culturally relative. Instead, she argues, "the author often encoded in the American Indian caricature ('caricature' because they are rarely well developed characters) his or her assumptions based on racial stereotypes, making the caricature a metonym for all American Indians" (1). Such stereotypes were widely spread in some of the Pocahontas narratives, as well as in other Romantic texts. Following the dichotomy presented at the end of the eighteenth century, the stereotypes in nineteenth century literature either portrayed Native Americans as naturalistic saints, as Rousseau's "noble savage", or as villains, as De Pauw's "degenerate race". Even though Gobineau's theories on the degeneration of races through miscegenation appeared only in 1853, some British authors had already written about it without really formulating a theory. Rev. Peter Fontaine of Virginia, for instance, in a letter written in 1757, clearly rejects intermarriage between Blacks and Whites, although accepting the possibility of mixing between whites and natives:

> But here methinks I can hear you observe, What! Englishmen intermarry with Indians? But I can convince you that they are guilty of

> much more heinous practices, more unjustifiable in the sight of God and man ... for many base wretches amongst us take up with negro women, by which means the country swarms with mulatto bastards, and these mulattoes, if but three generations removed from the black father or mother, may, by the indulgence of the laws of the country, intermarry with the white people, and actually do every day so marry. Now, if instead of this abominable practice which hath polluted the blood of many amongst us, we had taken Indian wives in the first place, it would have made them some compensation for their lands. They are a free people, and the offspring would not be born in a state of slavery. We should become rightful heirs of their lands, and should not have smutted our blood, for the Indian children when born are as white as Spanish or Portuguese. (350-351)

The economic interests behind Fontaine's discourse are quite clear in the passage above. His theory of the whitening of the Native American children was, as Tilton argues, very common at that time, so his suggestion is not for the "production" of a hybrid people, but for the assimilation of the Native American people into the white world. There is also a gender question in his text: white men are supposed to take native wives, but white women are not mentioned in such a context. As Rebecca Blevins Faery states, "white women, their bodies and their sexuality, [were] positioned as guardians of the boundaries of race to serve the territorial and political purpose of white men and their claim to dominance" (10). In "Pocahontas: the Malleability of Race or the Monster Miscegenation", Kendra Hamilton suggests that the dynamic of Fontaine's text could not be clearer: "the so-called Indian represents that which may be absorbed, the African, the abject matter which may not — or only at great peril" (5). Fontaine's ideas were not followed at all, and by the end of the eighteenth century Pocahontas's marriage was the great exception that confirmed the rule: laws against intermarriage were severe enough and the racial theories published in that period reinforced these laws and the racial prejudices inserted in them.

Thomas Jefferson had an opinion similar to Fontaine's. In 1808, in an attempt to convince some Native Americans of the suitability of adopting Anglo-

American laws and agricultural practices, the President told a visiting party of Delawares, Mohicans and Munries, "you will mix with us by marriage, your blood will run in our veins, and will spread with us over this great island" (Writings 452). He also wrote to Colonel Benjamin Hawkins (1803):

> the ultimate point of rest and happiness for them is to let our settlements and theirs meet and blend together, to intermix, and become one people. Incorporating themselves with us as citizens of the United States, this is what the natural progress of things will, of course, bring on, and it will be better to promote than to retard it (363)

In these two passages, the idea of the Native Americans as a vanishing race is quite clear, their only hope being in miscegenation with the white people. They are not supposed to be side by side with whites, but inside them, in their blood. It is possible to perceive, through these excerpts, that Jefferson believed that the blending and assimilation of one race into the other was a natural process, and that the Native Americans were in fact doomed to disappear. This was also Benjamin Franklin's opinion, who considered the natives' extermination a consequence of their love for rum, as it is possible to see in his *Autobiography*:

> And indeed if it be the design of Providence to extirpate these savages in order to make room for cultivators of the earth, it seems not improbable that rum may be the appointed means. It has already annihilated all the tribes who formerly inhabited the seacoast. (113)

Paul Finkelman, in "The Crime of Color", declares that from the very beginning of the colonial period there was an ambiguous way of treating Native Americans, sometimes worse than Blacks, for, while the African slaves were encouraged to survive and procreate for economic reasons, government policies encouraged the systematic destruction of the natives. Yet, he argues,

> in terms of the legal system's use of race, this led to some strange results. When not killing them or herding them into isolation on reservation, white America sometimes allowed and even encouraged at least some Indians to acculturate, and in effect, become whites. In the seventeenth century southerners usually saw the Indian as a 'savage beast', but

> a century later the Indian became a 'noble savage' who might be integrated into American society. (2065-2066)

In the same way, Jefferson saw the Native American as "noble savages", while revealing disdain and hatred for blacks. He wrote that blacks were "in reason much inferior" to Anglo-American, "and that in imagination they are dull, tasteless, and anomalous" (266). In contrast, he perceived that the Native Americans:

> will often carve figures on their pipes not destitute of design and merit. They will crayon out an animal, a plant, or a country, so as to prove the existence of a germ in their minds which only wants cultivation. They astonish you with strokes of the most sublime oratory; such as prove their reason and sentiment strong, their imagination glowing and elevated. But never yet could I find that a black had uttered a thought above the level of plain narration; never see even an elementary trait of painting or sculpture. ... Misery is often the parent of the most affecting touches in poetry. -- Among the blacks is misery enough, God knows, but no poetry. (*Notes* 266-67)

Although in late twentieth and early twenty-first centuries all these ideas on race have been replaced by theories on ethnicity, and some scientists, like the anthropologist Paul Gilroy, in *Against Race*, have even declared that races do not exist, it is quite important to understand the first theories on this complex subject so that it becomes easier to understand how literary texts, written when such theories were spreading, deal with questions of interracial relationships. For Bhabha, in *Location of Culture*, it is possible to read the racial stereotype of colonial discourse in terms of "fetishism"[10] (74). Bhabha defines the "fetish" as a concept that gives "access to an 'identity' which is predicted as much on mastery and pleasure as it is on anxiety and defense." The fetish, or stereotype, in Bhabha's reading, is a form of "multiple and contradictory beliefs in its recognition of difference and the disavowal of it" (*Location of Culture* 75). Bhabha elaborates on the function of the colonial stereotype by analogy with Freud's idea of the function that the fetish plays for the fetishist. The stereotype not only shares the fetish's metonymic structure of replacement for the 'real' thing but, like the fetish, it is a way of expressing and containing severely conflictual thoughts and positions. In Bhabha's gloss, "fetishism is always a 'play' or vacillation between the archaic affirmation of wholeness/ similarity... and the anxiety associated with lack and difference" (*Location of Culture* 74).

For Bhabha, this structure of emotional ambivalence on the part of the colonizer is partly manifested in a consistent pattern of conflict in colonial discourse. For instance, the colonized subject can be simultaneously beyond comprehension (as in stereotypes about 'the inscrutable Oriental' or 'the mysterious East') and yet completely predictable as the object of the all-seeing colonial look. Similarly the colonized subject can be

> both savage (cannibal) and yet the most obedient and dignified of servants (the bearer of food); he is the embodiment of rampant sexuality and yet innocent as a child; he is mystical, primitive, simple-minded and yet the most worldly and accomplished liar, and manipulator of social forces (*Location of Culture*, 82)

This ambivalence of feelings toward the natives is very similar to the dichotomy of "Noble Savage" *versus* "Bad Savage" already discussed. The difference is that in the fetish both the "good" and the "bad" characteristics occur at the same time. In literary texts of early nineteenth century, such ambivalence is clearly perceived, especially in the Pocahontas narratives, in which the native girl always confirms to the stereotype of the Good Indian, pure and innocent, but at the same time the embodiment of sexuality to the white men who fall in love with her.

As Bhabha argues, "the stereotype, as the primary point of subjectification in colonial discourse, for both colonizer and colonized, is the scene of a similar fantasy and defence — the desire for an originality which is again threatened by the differences of race, colour and culture" (*Location of Culture* 75). The stereotype, then, is not merely a simplification because it is a false representation of a known reality, it is a simplification because it is a rigid form of representation that, as Bhabha points out, "in denying the play of difference ... constitutes a problem for the *representation* of the subjected in signification of psychic and social relations" (*Location of Culture* 75 – emphasis in the original). The stereotype prevents the circulation and articulation of the meaning of "race" as anything other than its fixity in racism. It is common knowledge that Blacks are licentious, Asians duplicitous, Indians treacherous ...

To understand colonial discourse it is important to notice that its construction, as well as the exercise of colonial power through it, asks for an articulation of difference, both racial and sexual, whose object is "otherness", at the same time an object of desire and disdain. Bhabha also argues that an important feature of colonial discourse is "its dependence on the concept of 'fixity' in the ideological construction of otherness" (*Location of Culture* 66). Such a "fixity", the stereotype, symbolizes the cultural/historical/racial difference in the discourse of colonization, and is a very contradictory means of representation, for at the same time that it implies rigidity and a static order, it also suggests disorder, decadence and repetition. It is a rival of knowledge and identification that hesitates between what is already known and something that must be anxiously repeated in order to become true.

During the colonization process, Native American people, although perceived by the European white people as racially and culturally inferior, were, sometimes, very important to the establishment of a possible communication between the two peoples, serving as interpreters of their language and culture. Next, there is a discussion on the role of these people, and on their importance to the process of nationalization of the US.

2.3. LIMINAL FIGURES

Liminal figures, or border figures, share with their own people and with some other people a certain kind of knowledge necessary to both. In some historical periods such figures were very important to the establishment of a certain communication between their people and some other people they were in contact with, for they were usually cultural brokers, that is, people who, facilitating contact, communication, cultural exchange, and conflict resolution in the early colonial period, helped to establish a closer relationship between the two people. Such figures appeared frequently in moments of invasions and/or colonization, when cultural brokers were crucial to the colonizer's survival. Liminal figures were important during the process of European colonization in the Americas, when natives were frequently trained in the European's language in order to serve as interpreters between their people and the colonizers'.

Gloria Anzaldúa, in *Borderlands/La Frontera*, defines as border figures the people who live in a borderland, which she defines as "physically presented wherever two or more cultures edge each other, where people of different races occupy the same territory, where under, lower and middle and upper classes touch, where the space between two individuals shrinks with intimacy" (Preface). During the colonial period social figures, who served as mediators between the white settlers and the indigenous people, were crucial to the development of the white settlement. "Living in the border" either means that liminal figures during the colonization process lived physically outside their places, or, metaphorically, that they had no places to live: learning the other's language and customs in order to work as a kind of ambassador between their people and the strangers, such figures were torn between the two groups without belonging to either. Anzaldúa also describes borderlands as "a vague and undetermined place created by the emotional residue of an unnatural boundary. It is a constant state of transition" (5). Such a borderland is the space where transgressions occur, where the mediator figure of the colonization process stands, a hybrid place in which languages and customs intermingle. It is also, as Sandra Almeida argues in "Bodily Encounters", a "site in which standardized dichotomies are problematized and contradictions are unveiled and valorized" (117).

For Mary Louise Pratt, in *Imperial Eyes*, borderlands is the site where different cultures live, the "contact zone", which she defines as "the space where cultures meet, clash and grapple with each other, often in contexts of highly asymmetrical relations of power" (6-7). For Pratt, each culture — and its literary expressions — must be understood within the context of the contact zone. It is also important to realize that, due to the "highly asymmetrical relations" (7) (one culture being much stronger than the other), the dominant culture's perspectives, values, rules, and ways of expression seem normal and natural. Pratt's concept of the contact zone facilitates the understanding of the reasons why subordinate cultures feel invisible, why they feel such powerful pressures to be like (or assimilate to) the dominant culture, and why they need to be so resilient and inventive as they find ways to negotiate, to resist, or undermine the dominant culture.

Living in more than one culture, using at least two languages, and being acquainted with at least two totally different ways of seeing the world, the mediator figures of the colonial period were constantly torn between at least two different ways. As Trinh T. Minh-ha argues, in "Not You / Like You",

> The moment the insider steps out from the inside she's [he's] no longer a mere insider. She [he] necessarily looks in from the outside while also looking out from the inside. Not quite the same, not quite the other, she [he] stands in that undetermined threshold place where she constantly drifts in and out. Undercutting the inside/outside opposition, her [his] intervention is necessarily that of both not quite an insider and not quite an outsider. She [he] is, in other words, this

> inappropriate other or same who moves about with always at least two gestures: that of affirming 'I am like you' while persisting in her [his] difference and that of reminding 'I am different' while unsettling every definition of otherness arrived at. (932)

This is what may have happened to several Native Americans who were taken to Europe to learn the language of their conquerors in order to help them sometimes to fight his / her own people. Even when not taken overseas, the simple fact of leaving his/her people to live with the stranger, not always willingly, was certainly a hard experience.

According to Alden T. Vaughan, in "Sir Walter Raleigh's Indian Interpreters – 1584-1618", between 1584 and 1618, a great number of Native Americans crossed the Atlantic under the protection of Sir Walter Raleigh. During these thirty-five years, says Vaughan, about twenty American natives under his sponsorship were in England to "receive instruction in the English language and to impart knowledge useful for colonial enterprises"

(1). Most of them "sooner or later returned to their homelands, where many played key roles in England's early overseas ventures" (1). Nobody ever registered these natives' opinions, but some of them were quite well known: Manteo, the Roanoke colonists' interpreter-guide; Squanto, the Pilgrims' "special instrument"[11]; Tomachichi of the Yamacraws and Thayedanegea (Joseph Brant) of the Mohawks, diplomatic delegates to London. The use of Native Americans as mediators began with Columbus and was practiced by Portuguese, French and Spanish expeditions before Raleigh's time, as he almost certainly knew from written and oral accounts. Raleigh's emphasis on the teaching of the English language to the natives he brought to England shows that he may have recognized, from the very beginning, that language was, as Vaughan states, "an essential instrument of empire" (3). Without communication between his explorers and colonists, on the one hand, and the natives of the Roanoke and Guiana, on the other, viable British settlement would be difficult, perhaps impossible, to keep, and an effective exploration and exploitation of native territory would be very hard to maintain (3).

The liminal figures that helped to bridge the gap between Native American and Anglo American culture were not treated in the same way by the European people. Raleigh's mediators were the first of a great line of culture brokers, greatly differing from later types for the language training and for the location of that training, in England rather than in the US, and also for the temporary nature of their role as brokers. As Alden T. Vaughan argues,

> [i]n stark contrast to most Indian and Euroamerican intermediaries on subsequent cultural frontiers, the central experience for Raleigh's interpreters was an intense indoctrination at the seat of empire — an experience that proved extremely useful to Ralegh and his colleagues and must have profoundly altered, in a way the sparse early records rarely review, the lives of his many recruits (4).

Raleigh, as well as Thomas Hariot, wrote about their encounters with Native Americans that seemed to adopt Christian and European culture without being able to fully understand its meaning. Such natives vacillated between the Same and the Other, thus reinforcing the colonial discourse and, at the same time, subverting it. It is possible to describe such a phenomenon using Homi Bhabha's term "colonial mimicry", which he defines as "the desire for a performed, recognizable Other, as a subject of a difference that is almost the same, but not quite" (86). The colonizer thus asks colonized people to imitate him/her, to use his/her language, to embrace his/her religion and so forth. Hariot's text, *A Briefe and True Report of the New Found Land Of Virginia*, reveals the dependence of colonial power on the construction of a superstitious Other, for, as Sabine Schülting states in "Bringing this Monstrous Birth to the World's Light", "European knowledge depend[ed] on conceding only partial knowledge to the natives" (6). Keeping the natives ignorant would also keep their superstitions, helping the Europeans to show how superior they were for knowing more. At the same time, stimulating the natives' superstitions would also help Europeans to make use of such superstitions in their own profit.

The occurrence of mimicry, the "almost the same but not quite" of the colonial subjects, makes the relationship between Native Americans and Europeans an even more complex issue. In the words of Homi Bhabha: "the discourse of mimicry is constructed around an ambivalence; in order to be effective, mimicry must continually produce its slippage, its excess, its difference" (86). The liminal figure is, then, in Bhabha's terminology, a "mimic man", an "impossible object" whose presence or identity is not lost or suppressed but denied from the very beginning; "impossible" because of his/her liminality, this strange position in which he/she finds him/herself when in contact with the alien culture. The presence of these liminal figures, although very important in some historical moments, such as during the British colonization in the Americas, was not really perceived as important either to their own people or to the other, which makes their loss of identity stronger and easier to perceive in literary texts. A liminal figure, says Bhabha, has been exclusively constructed, being inappropriate to fulfill any other role in his/her relationship with the others. Hence colonized people, as inappropriate subjects for colonial discourse, have only a partial presence; they are predominantly the object of, but not the subject of, discourse (*Location of Culture* 86).

The linguistic intermediaries, so appreciated by Raleigh, who may have learned from Richard Hakluyt's warning, in "Discourse of Western Planting", that future English colonists "first learne the language of the people there adjoyninge" (2:215) were not so valued by subsequent English explorers, especially in New England coast and occasionally in Virginia, who freely admitted their violent tactics against the Native Americans.

Not all Native American mediators during the colonial period were men. Indeed, several women carried out this function, including Pocahontas, whose role as liminal figure during the first years of British settlement in the USA was crucial to the survival of the settlers and of the colony as a whole. In Chapter 3, there is a detailed discussion on her role as mediator, as well as on other historical and/or literary figures that had also carried out the same function.

Literary texts portray different kinds of liminal figures, these figures "in between" who do not belong anywhere, according to the roles they perform. Some of these liminal figures, either male or female, were abducted by the alien people before acquiring such "liminality". Some of these abductions produced the captivity narratives that are described below.

2.4. CAPTIVITY NARRATIVES

According to Richard Dorson, in *America Begins*, the history of national identity in the USA has been deeply affected by captivity narratives in which an individual is removed from his or her home and struggles to return. A standard definition of the "captivity narrative" can be that it is a narrative by a Euro American man/woman of a frontier settlement, who relates his/her capture by Native Americans, his/her experience in captivity, his/her escape and eventual restoration into his/her proper society (169-170).

According to Jone Johnson Lewis, in "Women Captive and Indian Captivity Narratives", these captivity narratives, when narrated by a female, "are part of the culture's definition of what a "proper woman" should be and do" (2). In these narratives, women are not treated as women "should" be, frequently witnessing the violent death of husbands, brothers and children, thus being unable to perform "normal" women's roles like protecting their own children, dressing neatly and cleanly or in the "proper" garments, or, which was worse in the Puritan perspective, unable to limit their sexual activity to marriage to the "appropriate" kind of man. They are forced into roles unusual for women, including the use of violence in their own defense or that of children, being subjected to physical challenges such as long journeys on foot, or to trickery by their captors. Even the fact that they published stories of their lives is a step outside "normal" women's behavior. Such narratives also served to perpetuate stereotypes of Native Americans and white settlers, and were part of the ongoing conflict between these groups as the colonists moved westward.

Richard Slotkin points out that captivity narratives carried in their core concepts of morality and theology, with which the ideas of Lewis are in total accordance. Such narratives, Slotkin goes on, were embedded in "extended sermons and the dramatic events were framed by the rigorous formality of Puritan logic and Puritan rhetoric" (66).

Slotkin also declares that, from the point of view of New England, to be a captive in Native American hands was almost sure to result in "spiritual and physical catastrophe" (98). The captives were either lost forever into the wilderness, or came back "half-Indianized", or became Catholic and stayed in Canada, or married some "Canadian half-breed" or "Indian slut", or became totally savage. In any of these cases, the captive was a soul entirely lost to the tents of the English Israel[12]. As for the portrayal of the Native Americans in such narratives, Slotkin points out that, from the Puritans' viewpoint, they were God's instruments for the punishment of His guilty people, a reversal of the missionary and war narratives in which whites are the means used by God for the salvation or destruction of the Native Americans (99).

Slotkin also argues that all the English settlers in New England had left their home to come to the New

World voluntarily. But none of them got as close to the wilderness as the captives, not even the missionaries, whose spiritual ties were with the white civilization no matter where they lived. For the captive, such ties were violently cut and the hope that they would be restored was very small. Being a victim of captivity in the wilderness was the most difficult, and, therefore, the noblest way of getting close to God's will in relation to one's soul's election or damnation. The captivity narratives were the ideal way to express this anxiety and to symbolically resolve it (100).

The first captivity narrative, however, is not of a white woman. In fact, it is not even of a woman: it is John Smith's narrative of his capture by the Algonquians, his rescue from death by Pocahontas and his release. There are some important differences between Smith's abduction and the ones that are narrated during the seventeenth and eighteenth centuries. First of all, Smith was neither abducted during a war nor during a native raid to a white settlement. Instead, he was exploring the woods in order to map the territory and find different natives to trade with them for their corn. Second, although his partners were killed, he did not suffer any injuries before being sent to the natives' leader Powhatan, and even his trial may have been, as suggested by Hulme, a "ritual of mock execution" (150). Third, he was set free with a minimum of demands from the natives' part, and became an important figure in future negotiations with the same natives that had abducted him, which indicates that a special kind of relationship had been established between him and his captors due, perhaps to the interference of Pocahontas. Thus, Smith's abduction cannot be considered as an archetype for the captivity narratives that follow his, for their context and situations are quite different. However, his narrative is certainly the prototype for any other narrative concerning his rescue and his relationship with Pocahontas.

The first captivity narrative in which the captive is a

woman is Ralph Hamor's narrative of Pocahontas's abduction and subsequent captivity among the white settlers in Jamestown. Nevertheless, the first captivity narrative in which the captive is a white Puritan woman is Mary Rowlandson's *The Sovereignty and Goodness of God, Together with the Faithfulness of His Promises Displayed: Being a narrative of the Captivity and Restauration of Mrs. Mary Rowlandson* (1682), a text considered by Slotkin and other critics like Scott B. Vickers as an archetype — that is, as the first of a genre of narrative within American culture, "the primary model of which all subsequent captivity are diminished copies, or types" (Slotkin 102). That narrative created a paradigm of individual and collective history that can be perceived as an informing structure all the way through Puritan and in later American narrative literature.

While the first captivity narratives in New England were firsthand accounts, like Mrs. Rowlandson's, or secondhand like Hannah Dustan's, whose captivity was narrated by Cotton Mather in *Magnalia Christi Americana* (1668), a demand for more narrative literature derived from experience in the American wilderness, and the increasing popularity of such narratives facilitated the fictionalization of stories with the fabrication of imaginary adventures, which led to a gradual acceptance of literary form as suitable means for reporting the American experience.

Rebecca Blevins Faery states that, in the popular culture of the US, conflicts between Native Americans and whites have "epic and archetypal dimensions and have served as a universal definition of American identity and history" (7). Throughout her study, Faery compares the white female captivity narratives with the story of the Native American female Pocahontas, also as a captive. She argues that

> The figures of the white woman captive and the young Native woman who welcomes and sustains colonial intruders into her country occupy opposite sides of the same discursive coin and have been partners in the ongoing

constructions of race, sex and national identity in the US. (9)

Stories of whites captured by Native Americans, especially those involving women, initiated what would become a persistent trope in articulations of racial difference in the US. As Faery points out, "[s]tories of Indian captivity are witness to the construction and operation of discourses of race in America — and witness as well to the ways women and their sexuality have been considered to serve those discourses" (10), especially racial discourses.

As Henry Louis Gates, Jr., says in *Loose Canons*, "Race is a text (an array of discursive practices), not an essence. It must be read with painstaking care and suspicion, not imbibed" (79). Thus, it is possible to see captivity tales as part of the discussion on the "text" of race in its particularly American aspect, having occupied an important place in that "array of discursive practices" that have constituted race and that Gates advises to be read with both "care and suspicion". Ruth Frankenberg writes, in *White Women, Race Matters*, that "[o]ne effect of colonial discourse is the production of an unmasked Other racial and cultural categories with which the racially and culturally dominant category is constructed" (17). Faery argues that, as categories, both whiteness and darkness did not exist until political convenience provoked their existence, which first appear in Spain, with prejudices against Jews and Moors, but most significantly in the North American colonies, as British colonists, along with other European settlers, demanded land, displacing the original inhabitants and bringing African labor for plantation (11). Of course, each people involved in the process of colonization were aware of their different appearances, but at the beginning of their relationship, cultural, and especially religious, differences were much more important than skin color.

The captivity narrative, that distinctively American genre, appeared and evolved more or less at the same time with the discourses that constituted the uniquely American version of racial difference. As Faery argues, "captivity narratives were very quickly recognized as useful instruments in the process of evoking 'race' and asserting racial hierarchy" (12). As such stories became more and more popular, and the fictional ones proliferated, their own textual "other", narratives on Pocahontas and other similar Native Americans "maidens", also moved toward and finally into the forefront of writing that occupied a public character in the process of building and defining a nation.

In the textual analysis in Chapter 3, my focus is on a fact that has usually been avoided and occluded in relation to Pocahontas's life: that she was herself abducted by the British and held hostage in Jamestown to protect the settlement from attack by her father and his warriors. The Native American girl certainly belongs to a history of captive women within the struggle between her people and the British colonists; indeed, the story of her imprisonment in Jamestown is the first story of a woman's captivity to be written into that long story, and she herself becomes a kind of predecessor and Native counterpart to Rowlandson, though a silenced one. Pocahontas's captivity can be seen as a native counterpart to Rowlandson in the sense that both were captured while at home, and both were used to achieve political and economical purposes: the first helped establish peace between her people and the whites, which favored the development of the tobacco plantation promoted by her white husband; the second, abducted during King Philip's war, served as unwilling intermediary between the British and the natives, and her ransom helped the natives support themselves during the war. As Faery points out, "[n]arratives of white women's captivities rest ... on precursor narratives of native women's captivities" (16). It is also important to be aware that the story of Pocahontas's captivity recorded in the records of the Jamestown settlement, with all its gaps and silences must stand in for other native women who were taken captive by conquerors and colonists but whose stories were never written at all. Although unwritten, these stories are known through the captors' narratives, who, like Cuneo, seem to be very proud of their act of violence.

Miscegenation, liminal figures and captivity narratives are very closely related to the construction of an American national identity. Racial and cultural prejudices, that have excluded Native Americans from the nation's "limitless future", have also provoked the birth of some liminal figures, people with mixed blood who were not accepted by either people. Although liminal figures were not always of mixed blood, these were considered the most dangerous, for not belonging, actually, anywhere. Some "pure-blood" natives or Europeans became liminal figures against their will, being abducted by the alien people and forced to learn the other's culture and language. These abductions gave origin to the captivity narratives that can be also seen as "liminal narratives", for they are informed by the encounters between cultures. Then, it is not really possible to treat any of these aspects in isolation when discussing the construction of a national American identity. They are discussed in different moments of the following chapter just to make the discussion easier to be understood.

3

ROMANTIC TEXTS ON POCAHONTAS AND THE CONSTRUCTION OF AN AMERICAN NATIONAL IDENTITY

> *Her people have passed away-most of their names are forgotten, but the name of Pocahontas, and the story of her generous deed, will ever be honored and remembered.*
>
> Harris Patton, A. M., Patton, Jacob Harris[1]

In order to discuss the literary texts about Pocahontas, I have divided this chapter into three parts, each dealing with one of the three themes that are pervasive throughout the texts. The first deals with the issue of miscegenation, a very important theme in early nineteenth century texts, either about Pocahontas or about other native characters. The second part deals with the liminal figures present in the literary texts I have analyzed, due to their importance to the establishment of a closer relationship between Europeans and Native Americans. Finally, the third part discusses the captivity narratives inserted in these texts as an important part to their understanding and the historical background in which they are inserted. These three parts, together, form a discussion about some of the literary texts about Pocahontas written during the years 1800 – 1860, establishing a kind of comparison between the Pocahontas narratives and the narratives of James Fenimore Cooper, whose texts are considered as founding narratives of the

American nation. I have also compared the Pocahontas narratives to two other novels, *Hobomok*, by Lydia Maria Child, and *Hope Leslie*, by Catherine Maria Sedwick.

3.1. "I MIGHT HAVE FORGOTTEN THAT NATURE HAD PUT BARRIERS BETWEEN US": MIXING RACES / MIXING BLOOD IN ROMANTIC NARRATIVES OF POCAHONTAS

> *Come, boyes, Virginia longs till we share the rest of her maiden-head.*
>
> George Chapman, Ben Jonson, John Marston [2]

> *... for the good of this plantation, for the honour of our countrie, for the glory of God, for my owne salvation, and for the conuerting to the true knowledge of God and Iesus Christ, an unbeleeuing creature, namely Pokahuntas.*
>
> John Rolfe [3]

> *John Rolfe is not our ancestor.*
> *We rise from out the soul of her*
> *Held in native wonderland,*
> *While the sun's rays kissed her hand,*
> *In the springtime,*
> In Virginia,
> *Our Mother, Pocahontas*
>
> Vachel Lindsay [4]

When discussing Pocahontas, whether as a historical or as a fictional character, it is impossible to avoid the theme of miscegenation, due to her marriage to John Rolfe and the birth of her son. Her story, which has become the American archetype[5] of the maiden princess who rescues the stranger and marries him, afterwards, is not that simple. Many people think she married John Smith, the British adventurer she supposedly saved, especially after the release of Disney's animation in 1995. However, in fact, she married another colonist seven years after the famous rescue. It is interesting to note that the romantic texts on her, especially the plays, just forgot this lapse of time and put the events all together. Her son is not always mentioned either. And her relationship with John Smith is portrayed, in some of them, as the most important event of her life. Comparing the texts on the Native American girl among themselves, one notices that these texts deal with the issue of interracial marriage in three ways: first, there is a certain condescendence towards the girl, so that her marriage to the white man is accepted, but there is not a single possibility of a white woman marrying a native man, for such would be "unnatural", as was proposed by the racial theories of Buffon and De Pauw[6]. A Native American woman was thought inferior, and had much to gain from such a marriage, while a white woman would suffer a loss, especially concerning her soul, for the natives were "heathens" and did not accept the Christian God. Besides, a native girl, in marrying a white man, would leave her people and go to the white world, assuming his customs and traditions. A second way of dealing with it is to accept the marriage of a white woman and a native man under the condition that they live either outside society or with the native people, so that the white people need not witness such an "unnatural" relationship. A third way of dealing with such a complex subject is by a total and complete rejection of such a union, no matter the gender of the people involved, but with an even stronger revulsion against it when the white partner is female. The point in comparing and/or contrasting such texts is to show how these writers establish similar and/or different ways of dealing with a love relationship between a Native-American and a white person in their attempt to find a place for the native in the "forgetting to remember" need for building a nation.

Nevertheless, it is necessary to understand that European thought concerning Native American people was not always the same. The first British to venture in the Americas looked upon the Algonquian people, the Native Americans who lived where now is Virginia, in an ambiguous way. At first, interracial marriage was not completely forbidden, for the Native Americans were not judged by their color, but by their culture. Thus, once natives accepted European religion and customs, marriage could be, to a certain extent, acceptable. Because the first contact between the British and the Algonquian people was friendly, the initial Anglo American view of the natives was largely favorable. As Alden T. Vaughan says in *Roots of American Racism*, imperial spokesmen of the early seventeenth century asserted that the natives of the Chesapeake Bay would "therefore welcome English outposts, willingly sell surplus land, engage in mutually profitable trade, and enthusiastically embrace Reformed Christianity" (22). Vaughan also states that there were no concerns about Native American color:

> early English writings reflect a deep bias against Indian culture but not against Indian color, shape, or features; the American native was socially deplorable but physically admirable. The challenge to English colonists was therefore educational: the natives must be converted to Protestant Christianity, taught English language and law, and trained in the social mores of Tudor-Stuart England. They must become Englishmen in everything except geographic origin. (13)

As the relationship between Anglo American and Native American changed, such a perception of the natives as similar to Europeans suffered a great transformation. Frequent hostilities from both sides corroded earlier

British views of the Native American. In Virginia, right after the Algonquian uprising of 1622, the natives started to be seen as "having little of humanity but shape", being "more brutish than the beast they hunt", and "naturally born slaves" (Purchas and John Boneil, qtd. by Vaughan *Roots* 23).

In New England the turning point was King Philip's war, during and after which the Native Americans were "monster shapt and fac'd like men", as Benjamin Tompson wrote in *New England Crisis* (1676: 19). Although animosities provoked by war did not really require a difference in color perception, for Vaughan, "the unconscious temptation to tar the Indian with the brush of physical inferiority — to differentiate and denigrate the enemy — appears to have been irresistible" (*Roots* 24). In this context Europeans became quite conscious of their own color. According to Theodore W. Allen, in *The Invention of the White Race*, the knowledge, ideologies, norms, and practices of whiteness and the concept of a "white race" were invented in the U.S. as part of a system of racial oppression designed to solve a particular problem in colonial Virginia. Prior to that time, although Europeans recognized differences in the color of human skin, they did not categorize themselves as white (Vaughan *Roots* 16-14).

In the late seventeenth and early eighteenth centuries several epithets for the natives' skin color appeared: "Tawny Pagans", "copper colour'd vermine" and, obviously, "redskins", due to their use of red paint on the warpath (Vaughan *Roots* 25). The possibility of interracial marriage between British Americans and natives became less and less acceptable. Religious and cultural differences became worse as differences in skin color seemed to deepen, especially after European naturalists, in a frantic attempt to classify all plant and animal life, also categorized human beings using their skin color to support their taxonomy, thus greatly contributing to the notion of Native Americans as inherently red and inferior.

In the late eighteenth century, when the US as a new nation was trying to establish an identity that would be typically American, the way to deal with the Native Americans in literature became ambiguous. After the War of Independence, and especially after the war of 1812, in which the United States tested its strength against other world powers, the new nation became concerned with building an idea of "America" that could go beyond the founding act of revolution and offering the future generations a source of national identity and legitimacy. Thus, a strong sense of nationalism was widely spread throughout the country, whose writers and intellectuals had been much influenced by the revolutionary ideals of freedom and equality. These writers, conscious that they were writing a new nation, looked for themes and ways of writing that would differentiate them from Europe. According to Scheckel, America would not achieve a

> true independence from Britain until they had

> produced a national literature and art that dealt with American materials, celebrated American history, illustrated and simultaneously shaped American character, thereby binding individual citizens together as a people through a shared vision of the nation and a national culture. (8)

In order to create a national literature, and forge a national American character, one of the ways American writers found was to look at the distant past: a past that Americans would not have without reinforcing their bonds to their European past. Instead of conceiving a past like that of the Europeans, Americans created an a-historical past. Rejecting European history, American writers started to look at the Native Americans' past, thus proposing it as the suitable matter for a national literature. Scheckel also states that connecting the natives with a remote past, together with "popular conceptions of their status as a dying race", transformed them into an "appealing romantic subject" (8). The natives would, then, represent a kind of pre-history of the American nation, giving the means to situate the nation's beginning in a distant a-historical past.

Thus, being transformed into an object of contemplation in nineteenth-century literature, the Native American image provided imaginative space for reflection on the meaning of national identity. This explains the huge amount of texts dealing with Native American characters in one way or another, such as the novels of James Fenimore Cooper, the popular plays with Native American themes, and the captivity narratives. Among the plays, some were about Pocahontas, the young native girl who allegedly saved the life of the English adventurer John Smith at the very beginning of American colonization, and who is also the theme of several novels and poems written in this period. However, using the natives as an important theme to literary texts did not mean accepting them as equal. On the contrary, the idea of mixing "white" and "red" races was not easily accepted.

According to Tilton, there is, in the romantic

narratives about Pocahontas, a constant fear of miscegenation, which may have made some authors change the order of events in her life or create a love relationship between the native girl and John Smith, thus avoiding her marriage to John Rolfe and the birth of their hybrid son. This fear arises almost at the beginning of the colonization, not only in relation to racial differences, but also to cultural and especially religious ones. As a very religious man, and conscious of breaking a cultural barrier, John Rolfe, while wishing to marry Pocahontas, wrote a letter to Governor Thomas Dale to ask his permission, explaining that such a marriage was "but for the good of this plantation, for the honour of our countrie, for the glory of God, for my owne salvation, and for the conuerting to the true knowledge of God and Iesus Christ, an unbeleeuing creature, namely Pokahuntas" (Hamor 63)[7]. Rolfe was certainly anxious to convince Governor Dale of his own appropriate intentions, as well as of the good that would come to the colony through this union, which would be worth running the risk of such a marriage.

In the romantic and pre-romantic narratives about Pocahontas, this fear of miscegenation was somehow hidden, or perhaps not seen as important, in the emphasis given to her relationship with John Smith, but when her marriage is mentioned, there are no obstacles due to their different races and cultures, because of an extreme condescendence toward Pocahontas, who is somehow whitened due to her behavior and her deeds toward the white people. All the authors included in this study see her as "the animated type of mercy and peace, unselfishness and truth" (Kritzer 322), thus deserving total approval from the British. This way, John Rolfe and his native bride usually have total support from their family and friends in each of the different texts, whose authors have found different ways of dealing with this matter, but none of them dismisses the figure of the native girl, always portrayed as the very guardian angel of the colonists. In John Davis's *Travels of four years and a half in the United States of America: during 1798, 1799, 1800, 1801, and 1802* (1803), she is introduced as a girl "whose soft simplicity and innocence cannot but hold captive every mind" (259). She is so "simple" and "innocent" that she falls in love with the first white man she sees:

> When Smith appeared before Powhatan, the first impression he made decided favourably for him on the minds of the women. This his knowledge of the sex soon discovered; but his attention was principally attracted by the charms of a young girl, whose looks emanated from a heart that was the seat of every tenderness, and who could not conceal those soft emotions of which the female bosom is so susceptible. It is in vain to attempt opposing the inroads of the blind god; the path of love is a path to which there is no end; in which there is no remedy for lovers but to give up their souls. (272)

Davis's description of the scene, in which Smith is taken before Powhatan, reminds that of Robertson concerning native women[8], who seem to be attracted by the stranger at first sight, which can be seen as a proof of white superiority, when the females of the "inferior" race prefer the white man to those of their own people[9]. It is this feeling that makes Pocahontas go against the will of her father, asking for Smith's life when he is to be executed.

> The women now became more bitter in their lamentations over the victim; but the savage Monarch was inexorable, and the executioners were lifting their arms to perform the office of death when *Pocahontas* ran with mournful distraction to the stone, and getting the victim's head into her arms, laid her own upon it to receive the blow. (273)

This romantic scene, in which Pocahontas acts like a true romantic heroine, risking her life to save her beloved, shows how she was turned from a living being into a representation of the good Indian type[10]. As Rayna Green notes, in "The Only Good Indian", this type of individual is an Indian who "acts as a friend to the white men, offering them aid, rescue, and spiritual and physical comfort even at the cost of his [/her] own life or status and comfort in his [/her] own tribe to do so. He [/she] saves white men from 'bad' Indians, and thus becomes a 'good' Indian" (382). So, the figure of Pocahontas becomes one of the great representations of the good Indian, as Tilton says: "her role as an actual mother and ancestor gave way to her persona as mythic protector, which she gained by demonstrations rather than procreation" (26).

Davis's portrayal of native women is based on the stereotype of exotic women as sensual and always willing to please men, no matter the race, although with a clear preference for whites. Describing the customs of Pocahontas's people, Davis says that it was part of their tradition that their leader, "when he was weary of his women", would give to a special guest one of them for a night, and that Powhatan decided to offer this honor to Smith, for whom he had "conceived a very high predilection" (274). With this decision, he calls two of his women and asks Smith to choose, thus describing the women's reaction:

> No sooner did this intelligence reach the ears of the squaws, than a bitter controversy took place between them respecting which of the two was the more worthy of pre-eminence. Jealousy cannot like other passions be

> restrained by modesty or prudence; a vent it will have; and soon it burst forth from these women with the impetuosity of a torrent. They had neither nails, nor fingers enough to scratch with; nor a volubility of tongue sufficient to deliver the abuse that laboured with convulsive throes to come forth from their bosoms. (274-75)

At least two readings of this scene are possible: first, that native women, or women in general, are just like children, who, instead of talking to solve their divergences, prefer to fight, so that the winner takes the reward. In a second reading, the native women's sexuality and their body seem to belong not to themselves, but to their husbands, who can dispose of them as they wish. Possessing the female bodies, that have always been connected to the earth itself, is a way of possessing the very land they live in. This is a very strong metaphor in the colonial period, when America as a whole was treated in sexual terms. As Rebecca Blevins Faery argues:

> Representing the New World as a "faire virgin" who was sexual fair game not only made possible and justified the plunder of the continents that were "new" to the Europeans

> who stumbled upon them; it also determined the roles European men and women would play in the colonial project, the treatment Native men and women were to receive at the hands of the colonizers, and the shape of the histories, stories, and legends that helped to engineer and define a nation of white European settlers in North America. Those who have clustered around the figure of Pocahontas are a pointed example. (101)

Ever since the first encounter between European people and the indigenous people of the American continent, Native American peoples were categorized into different stereotypes and naturally Native American women were no exception; they too were stereotyped and misconceptualised. As Meldan Tanrýsal argues, in "Squaws and Princesses or Corn Maidens: Misconceptions and Truths about Native American Women":

> On the one hand, the stereotypical Squaw image constituted the inferior, subservient, meek, lazy, wild and lustful woman. On the other hand, the stereotypical Princess was the guide, protector, helper, comforter, lover and rescuer of the white man. She fulfilled these roles at the cost of defying her people, changing her religion and even dying for the white man she loved. (1)

Davis does not avoid the theme of miscegenation, but his portrayal of the relationship of John Rolfe and Pocahontas is not presented as involving any danger to the white community. Nevertheless, Rolfe, even before marrying the native girl, had already isolated himself in a log-house in the woods, as if predicting his future life with his native wife, for mixed couples would usually live outside the settlements, as Tilton says, for "the white world ... was not yet ready to bear continual witness to such a joining" (79). John Rolfe is presented as "young, brave, generous, but of impetuous passions", and "accessible to softer emotions" (282-83), having fallen in love with Pocahontas just by knowing that she had "tender sentiments for Smith" (283). When they finally meet, at the imaginary grave of Smith, he cannot avoid telling her his feelings and dreams about her, who soon found herself also in love with the romantic settler, for, as Davis suggests, "[t]he breast of a woman is, perhaps, never more susceptible of a new passion than when it is agitated by the remains of a former one" (286). Getting Powhatan's consent, the couple was soon married, living in the place Rolfe had prepared for himself, outside the settlement. They had a son, whose name is not mentioned in Davis's text, and soon after his birth the novel ends. Her trip to England, her re-encounter with John Smith and her death in Gravesend do not take more than three pages. Davis clearly wished to show the native girl as a heroine of a romantic love story, and her role as mother and wife does not fit the pattern. Her son, mentioned just once, is soon forgotten. What really matters, in this novel, is that she is represented as the "Good Indian" always aware of white superiority and ready to risk her life to save and protect the stranger. According to Tilton, as I have already mentioned, it was Davis who first romanticized the Pocahontas story. Thus, the other romantic texts to be discussed may have been influenced by his. However, each one of them shows a different perspective on the question of miscegenation in the construction of an

American national identity. In Davis's novel, this question is not really presented as a problem, but the fact that the mixed couple lives outside the settlement is an indication of the concerns of the white world that would rather not have to face the possibility of miscegenation in any way, so, if necessary, the mixed couple and their possible offspring would live outside the towns, without disturbing the peace of the white settlement.

James Nelson Barker, in *The Indian Princess or La Belle Sauvage* (1808), introduces Pocahontas as having, from the very beginning, an aversion to some of her people's customs. Hunting, for instance, that is crucial to their very survival, is seen by the Princess[11] as a very sad practice that she herself wants to avoid:

> PRINCESS. O Nima! I will use my bow no longer; I go out to the wood, and my heart is light; but while my arrow flies, I sorrow; and when the bird drops through the branches, tears come into mine eyes. I will no longer use my bow. (124)

Thus, although she understands her father's reason for choosing her suitor from the Susquehannock nation, she rejects the idea of marrying him:

> PRINCESS ... Nima, the Susquehannocks are a powerful nation, and my father would have them for his friends. He gives his daughter to their prince, but his daughter trembles to look upon the fierce Miami. (124)

In "The Indian Princess", his introduction to Barker's play, Jeffrey H. Richards claims that Miami, Pocahontas's rejected fiancé, is not only the villain, but also a precursor of James Fenimore Cooper's Magua in *The Last of the Mohicans*, "who does not appear in Smith but whose name evokes a tribe that engineered a massacre of American soldiers in 1791" (111). The native maiden is easily charmed by Smith's appearance, although she does not fall in love with him as in Davis's text. But Pocahontas does not fall in love with the first white man she sees because Barker, changing the order of events, makes Smith and Rolfe come together to Virginia, a change that is also made by some other authors, like George Washington Parke Custis in *Pocahontas or the*

Settlers of Virginia (1855), and Charlotte Barnes in *The Forest Princess or Two Centuries Ago* (1848).

Smith in fact arrived in Virginia in 1607, as his own accounts and several other narratives state, for instance William Strachey's *The Historie of Travaile Into Virginia Britannia*, written in 1609. But John Rolfe was not in Virginia until 1610, after a problematic voyage from England in which he lost his wife and a newborn child. The date of his arrival in Virginia is not certain, but Mossiker states that he may have arrived there between 1610 to 1611, and a year or two later he was already known as a great tobacco planter (172-173). If Barker has John Smith and John Rolfe arriving at the same time in Virginia, that can be explained by the romantic ideal according to which a true romantic heroine may not fall in love more than once as Pocahontas does in Davis's text. Her meeting Smith and Rolfe almost at the same time prevents that situation and although she does save Smith's life, by warning the British settlement as a whole, she also saves Rolfe's life, following a romantic pattern in which the heroine marries the man she saves.

In Barker's text, Pocahontas is not the only one who greatly admires the British. Nantaquas, her brother, whom Smith has called in Generall Historie, "the most manliest, comeliest, boldest spirit, I ever saw in a Salvage" (236) is also astonished by how different from the natives the English Captain looks. When the young Native American, called Prince throughout the play, sees Smith for the first time, his reaction is that of a man before a supernatural being, a god, as he calls the British soldier:

> PRINCE. Sure 'tis our war-god, Aresqui himself, who lays our chiefs low! Now they stop; he fights no longer; he stands terrible as the panther, which the fearful hunter dares not approach. Stranger, brave stranger, Nantaquas must know thee! [music].
> He rushes out, and re-enters with SMITH.
> PRINCE. Art thou not then a God?
> SMITH. As thou art, warrior, but a man.
> PRINCE. Then art thou a man like a God, thou shalt be the brother of Nantaquas. Stranger, my father is king of the country, and many nations obey him: will thou be the friend of the great Powhatan? (125)

Below, there is a scene in which Nantaquas demonstrates, very clearly, how inferior he and his people are in relation to the white man whom he calls "brother":

> SMITH. Prince, the Great Spirit is the friend of the white men, and they have arts which the red men know not.
> PRINCE. My brother, will you teach the red men?
> SMITH. I come to do it. My king is a king of a mighty nation; he is great and good: go, said he, go and make the red men wise and happy. (126)

This is a representative moment: there is, in it, a clear distinction between the two warriors due to their skin color, one white and superior, the other red and to be subdued by the white. Although being willing to learn does not necessarily indicate inferiority, the fact that only the natives have something to learn in that relationship is significant.

Throughout the play there are long conversations among the Europeans about love as the most important feeling of their lives, but no one mentions the possibility of marrying one of the natives. Such a possibility is mentioned only after Pocahontas and Rolfe have met. But Rolfe is not the first white man she sees. Instead, she sees Smith when he is taken as prisoner by some of her father's men. The racial question is quite evident in this scene, beginning with Powhatan's and Pocahontas's words of admiration towards the soldier's appearance:

> POWHATAN. My people, strange beings have appeared among us; they come from the bosom of the waters, amid fire and thunder; one of them has our war-god delivered into our hands: behold the white being!
> Music. SMITH is brought in; his appearance excites universal wonder; POCAHONTAS expresses peculiar admiration.
> POCAHONTAS. O Nima! is it not a God! (131-32)

Pocahontas's feelings towards the stranger are of surprise and astonishment, but not love. She is to learn the meaning of love when she meets Rolfe afterwards. As for Miami, she totally despises him because he had almost killed Smith, whom she, following Nantaquas, calls "brother". When she meets John Rolfe they have a long conversation about their feelings, and once more it is clear that the British appearance is important to any native girl, and not only to Pocahontas. Nima, her friend, also falls in love with a white man, Robin, a foolish and cowardly man, whose words conquered the naïve girl. The play portrays two white women, Alice and Kate, who also came to the US in 1607. Historically, when the British sailed from England to settle down in Virginia, there were only males aboard. The first white women only came to the US two years later. In Barker's play, these two women are already married to white men and there is not a remote possibility of interracial relationship between white women and Native American men. Indeed, according to anti interracial marriage laws in Virginia, white men did not suffer any serious consequence for having sexual intercourse with Native American or Black women, for the offspring would inherit the mother's status, either free or slave. On the other hand, white women would suffer serious punishment. Thus, as Catherine Clinton and Michelle Gillespie say in "Introduction: Reflections on Sex, Race and Region", "[a]ccordingly, white women who engaged in interracial liaisons — especially females of the lower class — were subject[ed] increasingly to punishment through these laws, while white men were not" (xv). This is easily seen in the textual transcription of the law of 1691:

> That if any English woman being free shall have a bastard child by any negro or mulatto, she pay the sum of fifteen pounds sterling, within one month after such bastard child shall be born, to the Church wardens of the parish . . . and in default of such payment she shall be taken into the possession of the said Church wardens and disposed of for five yeares, and the said fine of fifteen pounds, or whatever the woman shall be disposed of for, shall be paid, one third part to their majesties . . . and one other third part to the use of the parish . . . and the other third part to the informer, and that such bastard child be bound out as a servant by the said Church wardens until he or she shall attain the age of thirty yeares, and in case such English woman that shall have such bastard child be a servant, she shall be sold by the said church wardens (after her time is expired that she ought by law serve her master), for five yeares, and the money

> she shall be sold for divided as if before appointed, and the child to serve as aforesaid. (Act XVI) [12]

Therefore, this text follows the first pattern I have described in the beginning of this chapter in which the relationship between white men and Native American women can be accepted, but not the other way around. The laws against interracial marriage, although beginning in the seventeenth century, still work in the nineteenth century, and are in accordance with early nineteenth century racial theories, in which the "white race" was considered superior, and in which miscegenation was seen as a cause of degeneration. Thus, avoiding interracial marriage was a way of avoiding miscegenation, keeping the white race pure and preserving white supremacy. The literary texts do not take into account illegal unions that gave birth to mixed-blood people. This way, they avoid miscegenation in literature also as a way to hide true miscegenation.

Pocahontas and John Rolfe do not marry in the play,

but when the play ends they are engaged. There is not a single mixed-blood character in the play, for the interracial marriage does not happen in the text. Avoiding the marriage and its consequences, Barker follows the pattern of romantic texts in which there are beautiful long suffering heroines who may eventually marry, but their married life is not usually portrayed in the text, not being part of the pattern of such a play.

This text, as well as the other plays, has a Native American male whose character is cruel and whose actions are evil; Miami, Pocahontas's native suitor, represents the "Bad Indian", contributing to the mythology of "Good Savage" versus "Bad Savage" in which Pocahontas's story is inscribed. Barker, just like Custis and Barnes after him, demonstrates in his play that the only Native American who deserves to live is the one who is whitened by his/her actions in helping the stranger. In his play, these "Good Indian" types are Pocahontas and her brother Nantaquas.

In Custis's play, *Pocahontas or the Settlers of Virginia* (1830), there are several moments when the problem of miscegenation is portrayed. At the beginning of the play, Custis presents Barclay, a white Englishman who has survived an earlier settlement in America. He is married to a native woman, Mantea, and they have some children, although there is no information about how many children they have. They live outside the native village, and do not move to the English settlement when it is established. Barclay is conscious of the strange position he is in, and demonstrates it when he decides to stay in Virginia instead of going back to England, where his offspring would not be accepted. As he says: "My children, altho' the offspring of an aboriginal mother, are dear to me, and so may it please your gracious pleasure, I would prefer to end my days in Virginia" (174).

In this play, Smith and Pocahontas do not have a love relationship. Rolfe is the first white man she sees, and he falls in love immediately. He cannot forget, however, that the girl is not European: "How full of grace and courtesy is this princess—savage, should I say" (177). In their second meeting, in Barclay's hut, Rolfe is charged with the protection of the girl on her way home, a task he does very well, like a true romantic hero. This way, he strengthens his bond to the girl and when she meets Smith she is already interested in Rolfe, whom she saves some time later, when her father plans to kill him and the English. As a true Good Indian type, she risks her life to save the life of the white man she already loves: "English Rolfe, I will save thee, or Pocahontas be no more" (185). The climax of the play is Smith's rescue, which comes at the end. After having asked her father to spare the prisoner's life, with humility and respect, Pocahontas gets angry and takes a position that is clearly against her father and her people:

> POCAHONTAS. *(Rising with dignity.)*
> Attend, but first to me. Cruel king, the ties of blood which bound me to thee are dissever'd, as have been long those of thy sanguinary religion; for know that I

have abjur'd thy senseless gods, and now worship the Supreme Being, the true Manitou, and the Father of the Universe; 't is his Almighty hand that sustains me, 't is his divine spirit that breathes in my soul, and prompts Pocahontas to a deed which future ages will admire.
(She rushes down from the throne, throws herself on the body of Smith, *raises he*r *arms, and calls to the executioners to "Strike"; they drop their weapons.* Powhatan *descends, raises up and embraces his daughter.)*
POWHATAN. I am subdued, unbind the prisoner. My child, my child. (191)

Already a Christian, for Barclay has introduced her to his Christian faith, and clearly performing the role of the Good Savage, whose deeds, which favored white men, are to be admired forever, Pocahontas is suitable to become Rolfe's wife, and Powhatan agrees. The play does not go farther, but Powhatan's last words, which close the play, are an indication of what the United States of America would become according to Custis:

Now it only remains for us to say, that looking thro' a long vista of futurity, to the time when these wild regions shall become the ancient and honour'd part of a great and glorious

American Empire, may we hope that when the tales of early days are told from the nursery, the library, or the stage, that kindly will be received the national story of *Pocahontas or The Settlement of Virginia*. (192)

Custis has Powhatan foresee the future of a "great American Empire" in which his people will be only the "ancient and honour'd part" of its "immemorial" past.

Barnes's play, *The Forest Princess, or Two Centuries Ago*, written in response to Custis's play, as Amelia Howe Kritzer states in her "Introduction", has a totally different plot, although it too deals with a white-native relationship. Miscegenation, as in Davis's novel, is not avoided, for she portrays Pocahontas's marriage to Rolfe as an important event in the native girl's life. The play is divided into three acts, each one representing a specific period. In the first one (1607), Pocahontas spares Smith's life in a clear act of rebellion against her father's will:

> POWHATAN (with terrible anger): Dare not speak again! He dies. Away! (*Goes up to his throne and raises his arm. At the*

> *same moment* Pocahontas *rushes to Smith, and clasps his head in her arms, laying her own head upon his, as the Indians are in the act of striking the blow.*)
> POCAHONTAS: (*Exclaims*). Then slay him thus!
> POWHATAN: Hold! Hold! (*The Indians pause.*) (*To* Pocahontas, *with surprise and admiration.*) Thou art a worthy daughter of thy race –
> A warrior's Spirit in a woman's form,
> Thou wilt not doubt the word of Powhatan.
> 'Tis pledged.
> (Pocahontas *relinquishes her grasp of Smith and comes forward.*)
> (*To the Indians*) Release the pale-face! (*They raise and unbind him.*) He is free!
> (Pocahontas *falls at the feet of* Powhatan *who stands upon his throne repelling* Smith's *expressions of gratitude. The Indians group around in wonder, and* Opachisco *points to the entrance, directing* Smith's *departure, as the curtain falls.*) (334)

In Act Two (1609), Pocahontas meets John Rolfe, who was already in love with her merely by hearing about her deeds. In their first meeting, he saves her from a panther, thus fitting the romantic pattern of heroism and making possible a love relationship between them. They then marry, and the act ends. Their son and their life together are not mentioned at this moment. The next act is in 1617, in London, where Pocahontas and Rolfe live in a comfortable house. Barnes breaks the pattern then: the mixed couple, the white man and the native woman, do not live apart from society. It is Pocahontas's turn to save her husband, who is accused of treachery for having married an Indian princess. Performing the role of a romantic heroine, Pocahontas, who is not quite healthy, goes beyond her strength in order to spare Rolfe's life. She succeeds, but she cannot hold on much longer. In a very romantic scene, she says farewell to her husband and dies.

> Pocahontas (*with a faint smile of joy*): That name! My own! the first by which thou knew'st me, love! 'Tis music to my soul. (Her trembling hands vainly attempt to lift the little chain from her neck. Her women raise it for her, and Pocahontas with fading sight and uncertain action at length casts it round Rolfe's neck.) I loose thee now. My eyes behold Virginia's grassy turf. I hear my father. Husband, fare thee well. We part, but we shall meet — above! (368)

Pocahontas's only son remains alive. However, as Tilton suggests, when the child of mixed couples, usually a male, survives, he will probably live in the white world, far from the traditions of his native ancestor (70).

Although Barnes shows a deep respect for Native Americans, it is a respect shown to someone who has already disappeared, or is close to it. She reinforces the idea that the natives belong to American history and literature, but only as part of that distant and immemorial past, which Anderson describes as being important in the construction of a nation. The native would belong nowhere, which makes the strategy of building a nation a very ambivalent one, as discussed by Bhabha, because the nation narrated by such texts emerges from an awareness that, despite the certainty with which the authors portray the Native Americans as part of the American past, they are still part of its present, although a non-willing and problematic presence in the construction of a national American identity at the beginning of the nineteenth century.

Sigourney's poem, "Pocahontas", also presents contradictory positions towards the natives. Although portraying Pocahontas's people as savage and hostile, it always compares the native girl to beautiful elements of American nature. She is a child when she saves Smith's life, but even though innocent and naive, she does not take long to perceive white superiority, helping the strangers in all possible ways:

> "The child! what madness fires her? Hence! Depart!
> Fly, daughter, fly! before the death-stroke rings;
> Divide her, warriors, from that English heart."
> In vain! for with convulsive grasp she clings:
> She claims a pardon from her frowning sire;
> Her pleading tones subdue his gather'd ire;
> And so, uplifting high his feathery dart,
> That doting father gave the child her will,
> And bade the victim live, and be his servant still. (XIX)

Her marriage to John Rolfe is not a surprise, for she seems to belong more to white people than to her own. She is Christianized before marrying, removing a serious obstacle in her way to wed the white colonist:

> In graceful youth, within the house of prayer,
> Who by the sacred font so humbly kneels,
> And with a tremulous yet earnest air,
> The deathless vow of Christian fealty seals?
> The Triune Name is breathed with hallow'd power,
> The dew baptismal bathes the forest-flower,
> And, lo her chasten'd smile that hope reveals
> Which nerved the weary dove o'er floods unbless'd
> The olive-leaf to pluck, and gain the ark of rest. (XXXI)

The other obstacle, savagery, is not a problem to her. She is presented, from the very first moment, as a noble person disguised in a copper skin body:

> A forest-child, amid the flowers at play!
> Her raven locks in strange profusion flowing;
> A sweet, wild girl, with eye of earnest ray,
> And olive cheek, at each emotion glowing;
> Yet, whether in her gladsome frolic leaping,
> Or 'neath the greenwood shade unconscious sleeping,
> Or with light oar her fairy pinnace rowing,
> Still, like the eaglet on its new-fledged wing,
> Her spirit glance bespoke the daughter of a king. (XVII)

In the same way the heroine dies in Barnes's play and in Davis's novel, so she dies in Sigourney's poem, leaving her only child with her husband. Her last words are directed not only to John Rolfe, but also to the English nation as a whole: "My hoarded love, my gratitude sincere,/ To thee and to thy people" (XLVII, 3-4).

From the discussion of these five narratives about Pocahontas, it is possible to draw certain conclusions: first, they all deal with miscegenation or the danger of it, but in none of them is this aspect of white-native relations really problematic, although the mixed couple, in Custis's play, is obliged to live outside society: Barclay and Mantea's marriage does not end in death or tragedy. Instead, when the play ends, they are happy together. An interesting point is that in this play Pocahontas and John Rolfe do not marry, they just become engaged. Avoiding the problem of miscegenation with his main characters, Custis presents, through Barclay and Mantea, the possibility of happiness in such marriages, which certainly goes against the standard established by most of the texts from that period. It is true that the texts in which

Pocahontas dies are all based on John Smith's *Generall Historie*, and thus their authors, trying to be faithful to that history, could not avoid her death. But while she was alive, her marriage to John Rolfe was portrayed as a happy one, without problems of acceptance by white society. As Tilton suggests, "the Powhatan[13] princess was always an exception: there was never any real possibility that in her marriage to Rolfe she could have served as an effective exemplar" (28).

As I have said in my introduction, besides the Pocahontas narratives I have analyzed two of James Fenimore Cooper's texts, *The Last of the Mohicans* and *The Pioneers*, in an attempt to show that the story of Pocahontas can be also included among the founding narratives of the U.S. nation, a status Cooper's narratives have already achieved. Reading Cooper's novels one notices that he presents a different idea concerning the issue of miscegenation, the aspect I have just discussed in five of the nineteenth century narratives about Pocahontas.

In Cooper's novels, the fear of miscegenation is present from the beginning of each one. Natty Bumppo, the main character of the Leatherstocking series, states about fifteen times, in *The Last of the Mohicans*, that he is a "man without a cross", and also finds other ways to make it clear to everybody that, although he lives in the woods and has a native as his best friend, he himself is white, with no mixed blood in his veins. In his construction of the Leatherstocking narrative, Cooper found no place for miscegenation. His strongest female character in this novel, Cora, is of mixed blood, a mulatto. She, the woman "with a cross", cannot have a happy fate. First, she is very aware of her condition, and always thinks of her sister, Alice, who is pure white, as a superior being. However, she is the oldest, and serves as a model to the youngest, who always listens to her, who protects and cares for Alice as if she were still a little child. Second, and most important in the decision of her end, she falls in love with a native man, Uncas, who requites her love. However, throughout the novel, they never talk about love or marriage. Their destiny is death, and only after that is there a reference to their possible love, made during their funeral by the girls of his nation, who conjured them to take care of one another in the "blessed hunting grounds of the Lenape" so that they would be "forever happy" (406).

But while the native girls believed in their future together in a kind of heaven, Natty, the only white man to understand their language, perceived the native girls' mistake and, "when they spoke of the future prospects of Cora and Uncas, he shook his head, like one who knew the error of their simple creed" (407). Not even after death is miscegenation allowed in the universe of Cooper's novels, for it would be against the establishment of a white nation that, although looking at the natives' past as the "family" history of the American nation, would prefer to see them as part of their past, not really belonging to the nation. The other couple of the novel, Alice Munro and Duncan Heyward, however, being white, have a very happy fate. As Wasserman states, Uncas, the noblest of all Cooper's natives, and Cora, of non-white ancestry, who fall in love with each other, cannot "cross the line", that is, can never cross the boundary that separates one race from the other, can never marry, for Cooper would never allow such a marriage. Their death is the only possible solution Cooper finds (175).

In this novel there is also the presence of the Good Indian versus the Bad Indian: Uncas, the young Mohican, and his father, Chingachgook, are examples of the first type, willing to help white people against other natives, although not really against their own people, for they are the last ones left. Magua, on the other hand, is a representative of the second type, who belongs to "a thievish race" and, as Natty puts it, "you can never make any thing of them but skulks and vagabonds" (43). However, unlike the Pocahontas narratives, the novels show no native females representing either one type or the other. Females in this novel are secondary characters, no matter how important they are to the course of the story.

In *The Pioneers*, there is no risk of miscegenation at all, for both the hero and the heroine are white. Nevertheless, while there is a suspicion that Oliver Edwards/Effingham is half Indian, his relationship with Elizabeth Temple could not be fulfilled. Their marriage and therefore their happiness are possible only because he was, after all, also a "man without a cross".

Comparing these texts to the Pocahontas narratives, it is possible to affirm that, in their attempt to establish a national American identity, the writers had to face a problem they would like to forget, the native people and all the violence they had suffered so that the American nation could emerge. In their will to forget in order to remember, as in the definition of a nation's essence pointed out by Renan, the possibility of a love relationship between natives and whites was certainly problematic. According to Renan, as I have discussed in Chapter 2, a nation, in order to construct its own identity, needs to forget the violence that has generated it, so that only the great heroic deeds will be remembered. In relation to Cooper's novels, such forgetting happens through the way the natives are described as belonging to a vanishing people, who will disappear due to their own fate, a people who were important in the past, but who cannot be important in the future, since they are doomed to disappear. Thus, the idea of a love relationship between any of them and a white man or woman is unacceptable, for such a relationship would be the white partner's condemnation. Probably aware of the racial theories of his time, especially the idea that a "mixed blood" people would inherit the worst of the two races, miscegenation is completely avoided in Cooper's novels. The Pocahontas narratives, as Leslie Fiedler suggests in *The Return of the Vanishing American*, embodies a possible reconciliation between white men and Native Americans (95), while Cooper's narratives totally avoid it. Such a possibility of reconciliation is due to Pocahontas's marriage to John Rolfe, a marriage that gave origin to one of the most influent families in Virginia. Cooper, however, does not allow a single possibility of such reconciliation in his novels, no matter how heroic the Native American is. Robert Berkhofer, in *The White Man's Indian*, confirms this view:

> Not only did Cooper subscribe to the contemporary tension between progress and simple nature, savagery and civilization, he also obeyed the romantic conventions of the novel of the time in not allowing an Indian, no matter how noble, to marry a White, and therefore no Indian could be a true hero in his novels if it meant wedding the heroine. (94)

Cooper's narratives, therefore, follow the third pattern I discussed at the beginning of this chapter, in which no kind of miscegenation is allowed. Interracial marriage, however, was considered by writers like Thomas Jefferson and Rev. Peter Fontaine, as a way of assimilating the natives into white society, without necessarily killing them. This way, the natives would certainly disappear. However, only white men are supposed to have female natives as wives, for women are supposed to adopt their husbands' way of living.

However, the Pocahontas narratives are not the only ones to give a kind of positive view of miscegenation. Lydia Maria Child's novel *Hobomok* is not totally opposed to it. Contrary to most of the texts, it is a white woman, Mary Conant, who decides to marry a Native American, Hobomok, who lives near Plymouth and who is considered by all the white people as a person of noble character:

> "I will be your wife, Hobomok, if you love me."
> "Hobomok has loved you many long moons," replied he; "but he loved like as he loves the Great Spirit."
> "Then meet me at my window an hour hence," said she, "and be ready to convey me to Plymouth." (161)

It is true that she was in a difficult moment of her life, feeling totally alone in the world, for her relationship with her father was very difficult, and her lover had just died in the West Indies. However, during the period they were married, which lasted three years, they were happy. She discovered that she could love that man who was so strange in his customs, but who loved her intensely. Following the pattern that established that mixed couples could not live in society, they lived in his wigwam near Plymouth, but they were not totally despised by their white neighbors. Sally Collier, who had always been Mary's best friend, visited her frequently, taking her little daughter with her, so that Little Hobomok and Little Mary could play together. However, this situation did not last. Hobomok discovered that Mary's first lover, Charles Brown, was alive, and renounced his own happiness so that his loved one could not only be happy, but also recover her place in the white world:

> the heart of Mary is not with the Indian. In her sleep she talks with the Great Spirit, and the name of the white man is on her lips. Hobomok will go far off among some of the red men in the west. They will dig him a grave, and Mary may sing the marriage song in the wigwam of the Englishman. (185)

Thus, a novel with an apparently different plot ends up filling the romantic pattern: the native parent is missing, and his son is to be educated as a white boy by his white mother and white stepfather. But Mary could never forget the biological father of her son, who would be forever remembered as a good friend and a noble character:

> But the devoted, romantic love of Hobomok was never forgotten by its object; and his faithful services to the "Yengees" are still remembered with gratitude; though the tender slip which he protected, has since become a mighty tree, and the nations of the earth seek refuge beneath its branches. (199)

The main difference between Hobomok and the Pocahontas narratives lies in the fact that the native is male, not female, and that he does not die. His son, however, has the same fate as Pocahontas's son in most of the texts, except in the ones in which he is not mentioned: he is to grow up as an English boy without knowing the customs and traditions of his native ancestor. In this text, the natives are also portrayed as a vanishing race, people who do not belong to the white world, not belonging to the nation either. The fact that Hobomok lives outside the town is a clear indication of how it is unacceptable for the white society to have natives around. The last scene in which Hobomok appears, going to the mountains and vanishing, is, in a certain way, a metaphor for the place his people would have in the following years: displaced by the white settlers, who would move farther and farther west, and not accepted by the white society, the only possible fate for Hobomok's people is to become part of the "immemorial past" of the U.S. nation without belonging to its "limitless future".

> Without trusting another look, he hurried forward. He paused on a neighboring hill, looked toward his wigwam till his strained vision could hardly discern the object, with a bursting heart again murmured his farewell and blessing, and forever passed away from New England (186)

Catherine Sedgwick, in her *Introduction* to *Hope Leslie*, compares the main Native American character, Magawisca, with Pocahontas. Indeed, there is a

Pocahontas-like scene in the novel, when the young Magawisca saves the life of her friend Everell Fletcher, who is captured by her father in the most tragic moment of the novel: Pequod Indians attack and kill Everell's mother, sisters and little brother in order to rescue Magawisca and Oneco who were living there after being captured by white soldiers. Mononotto, Magawisca's father, decides to kill Everell to avenge his son who had been killed by English soldiers. Magawisca, following the Pocahontas pattern, asks her father to spare the life of the young boy. The Pequod chief does not want to hear of it. Then the girl acts according to her feelings, risking her life to save his:

> At this moment a sun-beam penetrated the trees that enclosed the area, and fell athwart his brow and hair, kindling it with an almost supernatural brightness. To the savages, this was a token that the victim was accepted, and they sent forth a shout that rent the air. Everell bent forward, and pressed his forehead to the rock. The chief raised the deadly weapon, when Magawisca, springing from the precipitous side of the rock, screamed — "Forbear!" and interposed her arm. It was too

late. The blow was levelled--force and direction given--the stroke aimed at Everell's neck, severed his defender's arm, and left him unharmed. The lopped quivering member dropped over the precipice. Mononotto staggered and fell senseless, and all the savages, uttering horrible yells, rushed toward the fatal spot.
"Stand back!" cried Magawisca. "I have bought his life with my own. Fly, Everell--nay, speak not, but fly — thither — to the east!" she cried, more vehemently. (1:122)

Mutilated by her act, Magawisca knows she will never have Everell's love for several reasons: she refuses to become a Christian and to betray her father and her people. Her attitude toward Everell cannot be seen as treacherous, for the youth is not an actual enemy of her father. Thus, their fate is to live apart from each other, although Everell once said that he "might have forgotten that nature had put barriers between" them, and would love her (2: 57). Few days before he is abducted, his mother, conscious of the differences between her young boy and the Native American girl, writes his father a letter suggesting that they may be separated before they become adults, for

> To him she may be, and therefore it is, that innocent and safe as the intercourse of these children now is, it is for thee to decide whether it be not most wise to remove the maiden from our dwelling. Two young plants that have sprung up in close neighbourhood, may be separated while young; but if disjoined after their fibres are all intertwined, one, or perchance both, may perish. (41)

Although she likes her, the girl is not the daughter-in-law she would like to have; her son's wife could not be of that "savage people"; instead, she should be from a "Christian family" (40).

A very unconventional subplot in *Hope Leslie* is the happy union between Faith Leslie and Oneco. Faith, a white girl, Hope's sister, was abducted on the same tragic day Everell was. Due to Magawiska's attitude he was able to escape, but the girl remained with the natives, becoming one of them and ultimately marrying Magawisca's brother Oneco. It is true that they could not live among the white people, who would not accept their union, but among the Indians they seem to be all right. Like Barclay in Custis's play, Oneco and Faith do not suffer any really serious consequences for their marriage. Both Sedgwick's and Child's novels follow the second pattern I have already discussed, in which a Native American male marries a white female and the couple is not totally rejected by society once they live outside it.

From this analysis a series of conclusions can be pointed out. First, male-centered narratives, such as Cooper's novels, give more emphasis to white superiority. From the very beginning of his novels, Cooper strongly emphasizes white male characters as superior to the natives; second, female-centered narratives also present white supremacy, but in a less emphatic way. This supremacy, however, is shown not only through some white characters' attitudes in relation to the natives, but also in some native characters, who seem to consider themselves inferior for not being white; third, both kinds of texts are forced to face the "Indian problem" mentioned by Susan Schekel and emphasized by Robert Tilton. This problem, which has different aspects, concerns the place to be occupied by the natives in the construction of an American national identity. One of its aspects, perhaps the most problematic one, is the possibility of a love relationship between a Native American and a European, no matter who the male or the female partner is, although the situation becomes worse when the white partner is female. Because interracial marriages were legally forbidden, and the racial theories widely spread at the beginning of the nineteenth century were also against the mixing of races, the authors of the literary texts discussed in this chapter find different ways to deal with interracial relationships.

The Pocahontas narratives, for instance, although giving an altogether positive view of her marriage to John Rolfe, keep the romantic pattern in which the native parent is supposed to die, so that the offspring can be educated as a white person, without acquiring any of the native ancestor's customs and traditions. Of the five narratives about the Native American girl discussed in this dissertation, the only ones in which she does not die are Custis's and Barker's plays, which are also the ones in which she does not marry John Rolfe. In the ones she marries and has a son, she dies soon afterwards. Historically, she died when her son was about two or three years old, and he was indeed educated by his father's people. But besides trying to be historically accurate, which is not actually the main objective of these texts, the reason why she dies so young in them is because this is certainly the only way to follow the romantic pattern already discussed. This way, Pocahontas would belong to the "immemorial past" of the nation, always remembered as a great heroine because of her great deeds, but never to belong to the nation's "limitless future". The only possible way for the natives to become part of the nation would be through assimilation, with native females marrying white males and assuming the white way of living, having children and dying early, so that the children would not need to know anything about their native ancestors. Thus, the natives would belong to the nation in the memories of the white people, not in actual life.

James Fenimore Cooper's novels, on the other hand, deny any possibility of interracial union, denying also any possibilities of the natives being assimilated into the white world. The idea of the natives as a vanishing race is clearly portrayed in these narratives, in which they may belong to the nation's past, in which the natives who befriended the European will be remembered as a great but vanished people while the natives who were enemies to the European will be remembered as "savage beasts". None of them will take part in the nation's future, to which only the white people belong.

The novels of Catherine Maria Sedgwick and Lydia Maria Child, both female-centered narratives, can be seen as intermediary narratives, for they neither portray interracial unions as positively as the Pocahontas narratives do, not do they portray such unions as negatively as Cooper does. In both, *Hope Leslie* and *Hobomok*, there is a successful interracial marriage in which the female is white and the male is a native. In Hope Leslie, the mixed couple is formed by Faith Leslie and Oneco, who marry in the natives' village and live there happily ever after. In *Hobomok*, the couple is formed by Mary Conant and Hobomok, who marry according to the natives' laws and live happily for about three years. Their union ends because Mary's former lover comes back, and Hobomok goes to the mountains, releasing Mary from their marital bonds. However, these novels do not totally break the romantic pattern discussed in the beginning of this chapter: in *Hope Leslie* the mixed couple live happily because outside white society, and the white partner is considered lost to the white world, for she has "gone native". In *Hobomok*, the union ends because the novel needs to be fitted in the romantic pattern that says that when a child is born out of a mixed-blood union, the native partner is supposed to die so that the child can get an appropriate education. So, Hobomok has to leave, to vanish, so that Mary and his son could be accepted by the white society. Again, even when interracial unions are not portrayed negatively, they have to be either far from the white world or cannot last forever. In the process of building the US nation, such unions could only be possible in a mythical past, never to be allowed in the present day nation, even less in its future.

Before being romanticized by John Davis, the Pocahontas narratives of the seventeenth and eighteenth centuries assigned great importance to Pocahontas' marriage to John Rolfe, and some historians, like Robertson, have even suggested that the European should have married native women more often, so that the process of colonization would be less violent and traumatic. His ideas, however, were never put into practice, and, at the dawn of the nineteenth century nobody would take such ideas seriously. Miscegenation would have been a problem, not a solution, according to scientists like Corneille de Pauw and the Comte de Buffon, to whom the amalgamation of two different races would be very bad for both races, for the offspring would inherit only the worst traits of their parents. As Vaughan says, in *Roots*, "[i]n the first half of the nineteenth century, the basic options [concerning the natives] were assimilation or extermination, with removal to the West as a temporary stage in either case" (32). However, the biological solution was surpassed by laws against interracial marriages. As Vaughan goes on, "whatever the solution — miscegenation, allotment of farmlands in the East, removal to the West, or education in white-controlled boarding schools — the Indian was marked for gradual extinction" (32), an idea that is in accordance with the idea of the natives as a "vanishing people", with a very important past but without a future.

Thus, when Davis writes his novel on Pocahontas, *Travels of Four Years and a Half* (1803), he was probably aware of such "scientific" theories, and although he keeps her marriage in the story, it is not the most important event. And Pocahontas's marriage is the only interracial marriage portrayed in the novel. Other writers, like George Washington Parke Custis and James Nelson Barker, preferred to avoid such a complex and polemic theme, which is to be portrayed again by Charlotte Barnes and Lydia Sigourney. The event in itself is never portrayed negatively, but the fact that she dies soon after her son is born is quite romantic: she has to die so that her son can survive. In the newly formed American nation, to be the child of a native woman would be at least embarrassing, for all the ideas concerning Native Americans in the time the texts were published, especially the racial theories, portrayed them negatively. The only possible way a native would be able to belong to the white world of these authors would be by assimilating Europeans customs and adopting their religion.

As for the other romantic narratives, it is possible to conclude, after analyzing them, that the Native Americans are portrayed as an important part of the nation's mythical and glorious past, but that they can never really achieve an important role in present day nation, which makes it impossible to them to take part in the nation's vast future.

It is important to notice that some mixed-blood people became important liminal figures during the colonization process, and that some of the literary characters involved in interracial relationship can be also seen under this aspect. Next, there is a discussion concerning such literary characters in their role as liminal figures, and their importance to the construction of an American national identity.

3.2. Neither me, nor you, in between: Liminal figures in Romantic narratives on Pocahontas

> *She is like a guardian angel [who] watched over and preserved the infant colony which has developed into a great people, among whom her own descendants have ever been conspicuous for true nobility.*
>
> William Wirt Henry[14]

> *She would have done or suffered any thing to avert it — any thing but betray her father.*
>
> Catherine Maria Sedgwick[15]

> *Fly with the faithful youth, his steps to guide,*
> *Pierce the known thicket, breast the fordless tide,*
> *Illude the scout, avoid the ambush'd line,*
> *And lead him safely to his friends and thine;*
> *For thine shall be his friends, his heart, his name;*
> *His camp shall shout, his nation boast thy fame.*
>
> Joel Barlow[16]

In the same way the issue of miscegenation is very important to the construction of an American national identity, so is the presence of liminal figures who, in different ways, helped to establish a closer relationship between Native Americans and Europeans at the beginning of the colonization process, serving as mediators between their people and the strangers, many times helping to translate war tracts and political speeches, establishing a certain communication that sometimes was crucial to the survival of the people involved. Not every liminal figure is this way portrayed in literary texts. They are portrayed differently according to the roles they perform: first, there is the cultural broker, the most important kind of liminal figure for representing the contact between his/her culture and a completely different culture; second, there is the liminal figure who is either seen as a traitor or as a hero, depending on the point of view. Such is the case of a native, for instance, who is taught how to speak the European language and who is supposed to help the Europeans in contact with his/her people. However, instead of doing so, the native goes against the whites and leads his/her people to defend their own land. Seen as a traitor by the whites, he/she is certainly seen as a hero by his/her people. This kind of liminal figure is frequently characterized as a "Bad Indian", in opposition to the "Good Indian" type, who acts in precisely the opposite way. A third kind of liminal figure is the victim of abduction, someone who becomes a person "in between" cultures totally against his/her will, and who may become a cultural broker, or a traitor, or simply a victim, someone who is not able to act, allowing everybody else to act for him/her. And a fourth kind is the unimportant liminal figure, someone who is "in between" only for being in contact with two different cultures, but who does not interfere in any important action. The need to discuss such figures arises because some of them, acting as cultural brokers and/or traitors, interfere in the development of the narratives, and influence the behavior of the characters involved, changing the course of the plot and altering the end of the story. Their presence in the story can be an indication of how the author deals with such figures and how they may have or may not have influenced in the way he/she deals with the idea of a national identity. It is important to remember that some literary liminal figures are also historical characters that had important roles in the construction of national identity.

In this part of the dissertation, there is an analysis of different kinds of liminal figures both in the Pocahontas narratives as in the other romantic novels, to show the importance of such figures to the construction of an American national identity.

Liminal figures were of crucial importance for the colonial enterprise on the American continent since Columbus's voyage of 1492. Taken from their own people, not always willingly, native cultural brokers not only helped to establish close contact between their people and Europeans, but also helped the establishment of the new nations to come. As Anne Norton points out in *Reflections on Political Identity*:

> Liminars serve as mirrors for nations. At once other and like, they provide the occasion for the nation to constitute itself through reflection upon its identity. Their likeness permits contemplation and recognition, their difference the abstraction of those ideal traits that will henceforth define the nation. (54)

Liminal figures, however, are not always cultural brokers, as I have already pointed out. They are people who live between cultures, either helping in the relationship between the two people or not interfering at all. These "in between" places can be either geographically determined, as the borderlines between two countries, or linguistically and culturally established, as the boundaries between European colonizers and Native Americans.

Stephen Germic states that while external borders are usually connected with land and the real geography of the country, when these borders are aggressively overwhelmed what persists are internal borders. In the condition of being defeated by the colonizer, Native American nations could be located, after the arrival of the colonizers, only internally, by the common individual traits or language (Germic 337). Franz Fanon, in *Wretched*, implies a similar conception of internal and external borders when he writes that the space the colonized people occupy "is a world without spaciousness" (39), that is, a non-physical world. Or, as Fanon argues, "the colonized world is a world cut in two" (38), a world that is divided due to the delicate position the natives occupy, being displaced and having to accept, willingly or not, the power of the colonizer. Mediating people, therefore, became not only necessary, but absolutely indispensable for the colonial power from the beginning of the relationship, when the worlds of the European white and the Native American were totally unknown to each other, till the establishment of a new nation two centuries later, when the white people, who were no longer European, but American, decided to move westward in a new colonization process.

The most famous liminal figures of this type are female Native Americans who not only served as mediator figures between their own people and the colonizers, but helped the survival of the white outposts, bringing the white settlers food, serving as interpreters between the white people and their own people, sometimes preventing violent acts from both sides. In this part of the dissertation, before analyzing the literary texts in themselves, some comments on historical liminal figures are necessary for a better understanding of this complex issue.

Chronologically, the first of these liminal figures on the American continent is Malinche, from Mexico, also known as Doña Marina, or Malintzin, maybe Malinalli in her mother tongue. She was of crucial importance to Cortez from 1519, when she was given to him and baptized by Father Bartholomew de Olmedo, to 1527, when she died. No one knows exactly when she was born, but Frances E. Karttunen, in *Between Worlds*, situates her birth date around 1500. In 1522, she bore Cortez a son. In 1525, she was given in marriage to Juan Jaramillo, to whom she bore a daughter in 1526. She died in 1527, at approximately 27, and her both children were raised by Spanish stepmothers, following, in real life, the pattern presented by Tilton, in which the native parent dies young and the children have a white upbringing. According to Karttunen, a very important issue in the legend of Malinche is the fact that "the child born to Cortés and Doña Marina was the first mestizo,[17] the foundation of a new race and of the modern Mexican nation" (4). This "mestizo", who marks the beginning of a new race and of the modern Mexican nation, also marks the end of the native cultures and civilizations, and perhaps it is for this reason that, unlike the case of Pocahontas, whose descendants are very proud of her as an ancestor, Malinche is seen by the Mexican people as a traitor for having helped Cortez during the colonial enterprise. For being used by the Spanish conqueror as mistress as well as interpreter, she received another epithet: "La Chingada", the one who has been violated. But this does not diminish her guilt. As Cherríe Moraga states in "From a Long Line of Vendidas",

> [i]n the very act of intercourse with Cortez, Malinche is seen as having been violated. She is not, however, an innocent victim, but the guilty party, ultimately responsible for her own sexual victimization. Slavery and slander is the price she must pay for the pleasure our culture imagined she enjoyed. (185)

But Malinche is not always seen so negatively. She is also seen, as Karttunen points out, as the native intelligence incarnate, "the equal of the great Cortés, the person without whom he would have been led into traps and defeated" (3). Karttunen also says that Malinche represents the indigenous beauty that captivated the European conqueror, and that, in "folklore about Iztaccihuatl,[18] she goes to sleep rather than submit to being married, and as long as she sleeps, she protects her people" (3). She is, at the same time, La Malinche, the traitor of the Mexican people, and Iztaccihuatl, the sleeping woman who protects the same people. Between these two mythical conceptions of Doña Marina lies the Native American woman who, as Myra Jehlen states, in "Why Did the Europeans Cross the Ocean? A Seventeenth-Century Riddle", was "at once helpless and decisively powerful, victim of an oppressive gender and class system, yet also a significant agent in the defeat of her people" (57).

It is interesting to point out that, from the liminal figures discussed in this chapter, either historical or literary, only three are viewed so negatively: Malinche, who is rejected by her own people; Miami, in James Nelson Barker's *The Indian Princess*, who is rejected by the white people, by the Algonquians and also by his own people, the Susquehannocks; and Magua, in James Fennimore Cooper's *The Last of the Mohicans*, considered a great villain by the white people as well as by the Mohicans, for being a Huron, who were mortal enemies of the Mohicans. Magua was not rejected by his own people, who found in him a great leader in difficult times. Although the other liminal figures may also elicit different views, they are more positively portrayed. In the case of Malinche, as Gloria Anzaldúa says, in rejecting her, the Mexican people are in fact rejecting themselves. In her own words:

> Not me sold out my people but they me. *Malinali Tenepat,* or *Malintzin,* has become known as *la Chingada* — the fucked one. She has become the bad word that passes a dozen times a day from the lips of Chicanos. Whore, prostitute, the woman who sold her people out to the Spaniards are epithets Chicanos spit out with contempt.
> The worst kind of betrayal lies in making us believe that the Indian woman in us is the betrayer. We, *indias y mestizas,* police the Indian in us, brutalize and condemn her. Male culture has done a good job on us. Son *los costumbres que traicionan. La india en mí es la sombra: La Chingada, Tlazolteotl, Coatlicue. Son ellas que oyemos lamentando a sus hijas perdidas.* (22)

Paraguassú, a Tupinambá girl from present day Bahia, in Brazil, was also an important historical liminal figure. Her father, the cacique of the Tupinambás, gave her in marriage to a shipwrecked Portuguese mariner, Diego Alvarez Correa, who became famous among the natives under the name of Caramuru-Assu, or Creator of Fire. After some years of married life, Correa one day saw a European vessel approaching the Gulf of Bahia, and, suddenly taken by a longing for civilization, made signals to the ship. When he was leaving the shore in a boat that had been sent for him, he was discovered by Paraguassú, and without hesitation she swam after him and was kindly received on board of the vessel. Both landed in France and went on to Paris, where Queen Catherine de Medicis took great interest in the young Native American wife. Paraguassú quickly acquired civilized customs, was instructed in the Christian religion, and baptized under the name of Catherine Alvarez, the queen being her godmother. They returned to Brazil, and settled among the Tupinambás, near the site of the present town of Velha, where Correa acquired great influence on the tribe.

Paraguassú, with her countrymen, aided the first Portuguese settlers, and convinced the Tupinambás to submit without great resistance to foreign dominion. The territory of the Tupinambá nation was included in the grant of one of the twelve original hereditary captaincies, created in 1532, and the grantee, Pereira Coutinho, wishing to usurp the cultivated land around Velha, imprisoned Correa on a false charge. Paraguassú immediately roused her people, marched at their head against Coutinho, and defeated his forces, and the captain and his son perished in the battle. The governor-general of Brazil, Duarte da Costa, informed of Coutinho's injustice and fearing the influence of Paraguassú over her tribe, thought it prudent not to disturb her. She lived for long years with her husband and family at Velha, where in 1582 she founded the first church, dedicating it to Our Lady of Oracia. She was buried there, but the year of her death is uncertain.

There is no way to know how the Brazilian Native

American girl was seen by her people, for they were totally assimilated into the white society. But there is no doubt that her role as cultural broker between her people and her husband's people was crucial to the solid establishment of the Portuguese settlement in Bahia. It is amazing that though she left so many offspring, no one nowadays claims to be her descendant. David Treece, in *Exiles, Allies, Rebels*, however, considers her as the "legendary mother of the Colony" (95). He establishes a close relation between one of the literary texts on her, Ladislau do Santos Titara's poem *Paraguassú*, and the building of a Brazilian national identity after Independence. He states that she represents "the mythology of a heroic indigenous ancestry and of a shared tradition of anticolonial military resistance, through which the Brazilian national and the Indian could be identified as partners in a natural alliance" (96). He also argues that

> The symbolic usefulness of this mythology to the invention of a nationalist tradition is all the more striking when one remembers that, by

comparison with the violence of the national liberation struggles elsewhere in the Americas, Brazil could hardly be described as fighting an independence war as such. (96)

As for literary characters, these liminal figures appear in the texts to be discussed throughout this chapter in three different ways: they are usually young Native American females, who put themselves between their people and the stranger's, usually helping the European for detriment of their own, representing the "Good Indian" types — Pocahontas, in all the texts about her, and Magawisca, in *Hope Leslie* (1827). They may also be Native American males, who can represent either the "Good Indian" or the "Bad Indian" types — Nantaquas (who appears in several of the Pocahontas narratives), Miami (in Barker's play), Magua and Uncas (in *The Last of the Mohicans* (1826)), Hobomok (in Child's text). They are either female or male, with mixed ancestry, acting not always between both peoples, but always favoring the white relatives — Cora (in *The Last of the Mohicans*). Of course there are characters that do not fit in any of the types described above, like Barclay and Medea (in Custis's play), Natty Bumppo (in *The Last of the Mohicans*), Nelema and Faith (in *Hope Leslie*), and Mary (in *Hobomok* (1824)).

In Davis's *Travels of Four Years and a Half* (1803), the main cultural broker is Pocahontas. She is used by both her father and the white people as an interpreter and mediator, thus saving the white settlement from starving several times, as the following excerpt shows:

> The Colonists, therefore, thought once more of maintaining the fort; and in this resolution they were confirmed by the coming of Pocahontas with a numerous train of attendants, loaded with Indian corn and other grain of the country.
> The Colonists flocked with eager curiosity to behold an Indian girl, who had saved by her interposition the life of their Chief; nor was their admiration less excited by the beauty of her person, than the humanity of her disposition. (277)

She warned the whites against a plot by Powhatan against them, this time acting like Malinche, who, although forced to live with Europeans, helped them without hesitation. Davis narrates how the Algonquian girl warned the British settlers:

> The oldest warriors were posted in ambush to wage among them unseen destruction; and the whole party would inevitably have been destroyed by the Indians, had not the kind, the faithful, the lovely Pocahontas, in a dismal night of thunder, lightning, and rain, stole through the woods, and apprized Smith of his danger.
> Can the wild legends of rude ages, or the sentimental fictions of refinement, supply an heroine whose qualities would not be eclipsed by the Indian Pocahontas? (279)

The question at the end is a good indication of romantic feelings towards the Native American heroine. Besides Pocahontas, her brother Nantaquas also served as mediator, when she was captive in Jamestown. The use of such liminal figures to negotiate the ransom of captives was very common, like Pocahontas in Smith's *Generall Historie* (1624).

> And thus they all agreed in one point, they were directed onely by Powhatan to obtaine him our weapons, to cut our owne throats, with the manner where, how, and when, which

> we plainly found most true and apparant: yet he sent his messengers, and his dearest daughter Pocahontas with presents to excuse him of the injuries done by some rash untoward Captaines his subjects, desiring their liberties for this time, with the assurance of his love for ever. After Smith had given the prisoners what correction he thought fit, used them well a day or two after, & then delivered them Pocahontas, for whose sake onely he fayned to have saved their lives, and gave them libertie. (112) [19]

In Davis's text, Pocahontas's role as mediating figure ends right after her marriage, for she goes to Europe and dies soon after. In her actual life, however, even married to a white man, or maybe because of that, she was still a cultural broker, serving as an intermediary between her husband's people and her own when necessary. Because of her marriage, years of peace were achieved, which allowed the white colony to develop quickly.[20]

It is important to remember that, in deciding to help the stranger against her father's will, in Davis's text, Pocahontas puts herself in the position mentioned by

Trinh T. Minh-ha, neither inside, nor outside, at the same time an insider and an outsider, a liminal figure living in that vague space discussed by Anzaldúa. The fact that Rolfe has built a house outside the white settlement also puts him, from the very beginning, in an intermediary position, which facilitates his involvement with the girl. Both have become, then, liminal figures, belonging neither to one world nor to the other.

Barker's play, *The Indian Princess* (1808), presents two important cultural brokers, Pocahontas and her brother Nantaquas, for both help the British settlement and are willing to learn from the strangers, whom Barker portrays as considering the white as superior beings:

> NANTAQUAS. O priest, thou hast dreamed a false dream; Miami, thou tellest the tale that is not. Hearken, my father, to my true words! the white man is beloved by the Great Spirit; his king is like you, my father, good and great; and he comes from a land beyond the wide water, to make us wise and happy! (133)

Another liminal figure, though of a different type, is

Miami, Pocahontas's native suitor who puts himself between his own people, the Susquehannocks, and his lover's people, the Algonquians. When rejected by Pocahontas, he changes from a great hunter and warrior to the worst villain, ready to face Powhatan himself in order to assure what he considers his rights. In his anger he literally crosses the boundary between that "natural goodness" the "natural man" is supposed to have in Rousseau's terms to the "natural degeneracy" described by Buffon. Because of his attitude, he no longer belongs either to his own people, who cannot understand his actions, or to Pocahontas's people, who reject him totally. This way, unable to achieve his goals of killing the white people and taking Pocahontas to his village, his only suitable end is death:

> SMITH. Wretched king! what fiend could urge you?
> POWHATAN. Shame ties the tongue of Powhatan. Ask of that fiend-like priest, how, to please the angry Spirit, I was to massacre my friends.

> SMITH. Holy Religion! still beneath the veil of sacred piety what crimes lie hid! Bear hence that monster. Thou ferocious prince—
> MIAMI. Miami's tortures shall not feast your eyes!
> [Stabbing himself]
> SMITH. Rash youth, thou mightst have liv'd—
> MIAMI. Liv'd! man, look there!
> [Pointing to ROLFE and PRINCESS. He is borne off.] (162)

As Jeffrey H. Richards says in his introduction to Barker's play,

> The play ends, then, with a justification of white assimilation and obliteration of Native characteristics. The only good Indian, the play announces, is a whitened, acculturated one. The savage must die or retreat before European might or else face the erotic conversion of Native women into love objects and symbols of European possession of the land. (111)

Such assimilation, briefly discussed before, would be necessary so that the natives would vanish in a certain period of time, and would not belong to the nation's future, being part only of the unforgettable past of the nation. This idea of "whitened" native is also a pervasive theme in the romantic visual representations of Pocahontas, as I demonstrate in Chapter 4.

In Custis's play, *Pocahontas, or the Settlers of Virginia* (1830), there are several liminal figures of different kinds. Barclay, for instance, is the only survivor of the early Roanoke colony. Probably because he is the only white person in Virginia, he marries a Native American woman, Mantea. They live in a house outside the Algonquian village, and it is he who acts as an intermediary between the newcomers and the natives. Both he and his wife live in the contact zone, neither in one world nor in the other. And both serve as cultural brokers between one people and the other. Both have acquired that unique position in which they are neither insiders nor outsiders, being both things at the same time. Barclay's position is even seen as dubious for the ambivalent situation he is in, a white man who is almost "going native", a fear the European have in relation to either whites or native intermediaries. Many cultural brokers have suffered this kind of suspicion for living in between worlds:

> WEST: I do not much like this renegado.
> SMITH: By my faith, Master West, but we are of the condition of the host, who having but one flaggon for the use of all his guests, must serve peer, and peasant alike; now be our thirst for intelligence ever so great, we must drink from this renegado, our only cup. (174-75)

Other important liminal figures are Pocahontas and Namoutac. The Algonquian girl, due to her friendly relationship to Mantea, has already been introduced to Christianity, and sees her own people as inferior:

> POCAHONTAS: Matacoran is brave, yet he lacks the best attribute of courage—mercy. Since the light of the Christian doctrine has shone on my before benighted soul, I have learn'd that mercy is one of the attributes of the divinity I now adore, to good father Barclay I owe the knowledge which I have acquir'd of the only true God, whose worship I in secret perform; and rather than be the bride of that fierce and vindictive prince, I would fly to the depths of the forests, and take up my abode with the panther. (175-76)

Already in an "in between" position, the only path that

opens to Pocahontas, in the play, is to marry the stranger with whom she falls in love, the British adventurer John Rolfe. Still in Custis's play, Namoutac is a Native American who has gone to Europe with the British years before, during the foundation of the lost Roanoke colony. Although under a different name, Namoutac may be Manteo, one of the Native Americans who were taken to England from Roanoke Island and the lower Chesapeake Bay between 1584 to 1603 by Sir Walter Raleigh, as is attested by Vaughan in "Sir Walter Ralegh" (1). If Pocahontas at first feels torn between two religions, Namoutac is literally torn between two worlds. Although very happy to be again an "Indian", he is astonished by so many wonders he has seen, by the persons he has met, by the splendors of Europe, by the "pomp and pageantry of England". The passage below shows how happy he is at becoming an "Indian" again:

> NAMOUTAC: The sun shines for the last time upon Namoutac the English. Its morning beams will cheer him while

> roaming in his native forests, seeking the favourite haunts of his youth, dress'd in the garb of his country, his limbs will again become vigorous and elastic, he will be as swift as the deer of the hills, his heart will be as light as the feathers of his plumes; such will soon be Namoutac the Indian. Namoutac the English will be no more. (176)

However, when he decides to woo Omaya, a girl of his nation, he decides to act "after the manner of love affairs, of which I [Namoutac] have heard report in thy {English} country" (182). Like Barclay, he is also, at a point, suspected of treachery:

> ROLFE: Rascal, in my country where love affairs are conducted by treachery and outrage to the female parties, they end in the death of the traitors. Now you have play'd your part in this love affair, I shall play mine by shooting your thro' the head.   (presenting the pistol)
> OMAYA: Oh, good Sir Cavalier, do spare poor Namoutac; his travels have turn'd his brains — he would not have behav'd so when he was only an Indian. (182)

Omaya's words are a reference to Namoutac's position as liminal figure, as someone who lives in between, someone torn between two worlds.

Barnes's text *The Forest Princess* (1848) situates both Pocahontas and the villain Volday, a Swiss man, as liminal figures of different types: Pocahontas represents the mediator between her people and the stranger, who provides the settlement with food and useful information about life in the wilderness; Volday, European but not British, though part of the white settlement, is a stranger to both the British and the Algonquian peoples. While Pocahontas is, as Benson J. Lossing says in Our Country, "the guardian angel of the settlers" (193), Volday is a foolish white man who betrays the British in order to be, as he himself says "rewarded, honored by the savages, in time in lawless luxury may live and reign amid these forests" (337).

Risking her life to save the white men, the heroine of Barnes's text crosses the cultural border between her people and Europeans, a crossing that becomes complete when she marries Rolfe and goes to the white world, leaving her own behind. In London, her role as a mediator figure is a little different: instead of mediating between different peoples, she mediates two different views of the world, her husband's and the king's, who has sent Rolfe to prison for marrying a princess, thus situating Rolfe himself in between, a commoner who is not a commoner any more, but who is not a nobleman either. It is through her intervention that Rolfe survives, but at great cost, for she dies, just like the actual Pocahontas, at a very early age. But her death was not in vain: by saving her husband she has guaranteed her son's survival, so that she will not be forgotten.

Barnes makes Volday indeed a traitor. Coming to Virginia with the British, the German / Swiss man prepares an entrapment in act two in order to provoke a war between the natives and his fellowmen. His plans fail, and he goes to England, where he writes an anonymous letter to King James, accusing Rolfe of treachery, of intending to be the King of Virginia after Powhatan's death, using his marriage to the Indian Chief's daughter

American Identity and the Myth of Pocahontas

for that purpose. It is his letter that leads the King to send Rolfe to prison, an act that results in Pocahontas's death. The fact that the villain is a German is suggestive, for this way the author avoids establishing the British as well as the natives as evil persons, and all the blame goes to the German man. Volday represents the worst fear about concerning the relationship between white settlers and natives: the idea of being betrayed by someone of their own race, a white person who would help the natives instead of helping his/her own people. However, the intentions of the German man were to favor himself, not anybody else.

Sigourney's poem "Pocahontas" (1841) also portrays her as a liminal figure that places herself between her world and the stranger's, identifying herself more with the white world than with her own. In the poem, knowing that the settlers were in danger of starvation, Pocahontas took them provisions for the whole winter:

> Nor yet for this alone shall history's scroll

> Embalm thine image with a grateful tear;
> For when the grasp of famine tried the soul,
> When strength decay'd, and dark despair was near,
> Who led her train of playmates, day by day,
> O'er rock, and stream, and wild, a weary way,
> Their baskets teeming with the golden ear?
> Whose generous hand vouchsafed its tireless aid
> To guard a nation's germ? Thine, thine, heroic maid! (XXII)

Just like many other tales of Pocahontas, Sigourney's also has Pocahontas saving the whites from death by warning them against her father's plan, becoming, this way, the outsider who tries to be insider or vice-versa, belonging to neither world.

> Up, up-away! I heard the words of power,
> Those secret vows that seal a nation's doom,
> Bid the red flame burst forth at midnight hour,
> And make th' unconscious slumberer's bed his tomb,
> Spare not the babe-the rose leaf of a day
> But shred the sapling, like the oak, away.
> I heard the curse! My soul is sick with gloom:
> Wake, chieftains, wake! avert the hour of dread!"
> And with that warning voice the guardian-angel fled. (XXVI)

Her crossing to the Christian faith and her marriage to

Rolfe makes her even more liminal, neither a European nor a Native American, someone in between.

In Cooper's novels *The Last of the Mohicans* (1826) and *The Pioneers* (1823), the most important cultural broker is also the main character of both novels, the "man without a cross", Natty Bumppo, who shares with his Native American friend what he considers the best thing of the natives' way of living while at the same time assuring everybody that he is a white man. However, he does not belong to the white world any more, since he is much more used to living in the wilderness than in towns. He is an insider / outsider in relation to both worlds. The following scene shows how, even though he is white, Natty behaves like a native in the eyes of other white people, as, for instance, when Duncan Heyward, a white captain who was escorting Colonel Munro's daughters Cora and Alice, as well as the girls themselves, meet him for the first time:

> Heyward, and his female companions,

> witnessed this mysterious movement with secret uneasiness; for, though the conduct of the white man had hitherto been above reproach, his rude equipments, blunt address, and strong antipathies, together with the character of his silent associates, were all causes for exciting distrust in minds that had been so recently alarmed by Indian treachery. The stranger alone disregarded the passing incidents. He seated himself on a projection of the rocks, whence he gave no other signs of consciousness, than by the struggles of his spirit, as manifested in frequent and heavy sighs. Smothered voices were next heard, as though men called to each other in the bowels of the earth, when a sudden light flashed upon the vision of those without, and laid bare the much prized secret of the place. (*Last of the Mohicans* 60)

As Slotkin says, in the Leatherstocking tales there is a clear concern with the problematic character of the frontiersman, the border figure of Natty Bumppo: "the troubling blend of European, American and Indian elements that made him both a figure of promise and a nightmare to Cooper's contemporaries" (493). According to Renata Wasserman, "Natty's whiteness and his strict code of values, on one hand, the redness of his skin and his woodsman's craft, on the other, characterize him as a mediator between the social and the natural, the village and the forest, the law of society and the law of nature" (173). She also says that Natty's position as mediating figure is the most important one in the Leather-stocking series because "Cooper believes that the rules governing whites and Indians are different by nature" (174). Natty, for instance, does not consider the natives as inhuman, but humans from a different kind. He is, as Wasserman states, the character "closest to the white-native boundary on the white side". However, there is a "line drawn by color and religion that cannot be crossed, especially through marriage" (174).

Another very important liminal figure in *The Last of the Mohicans* (1826) is Cora, the only character of mixed blood in the novel. She is conscious of not belonging anywhere, although most of the people do not know her origin. She is concerned about skin color not only in relation to her own color, but also to the Native Americans she eventually meets. She asks "[s]hould we distrust the man because his manners are not our manners, and that his skin is dark?" (24). She considers herself cursed and inferior to her sister, who is totally white. She justifies her seriousness:

> 'That I cannot see the sunny side of the picture of life, like this artless but ardent enthusiast,' she added, laying her hand lightly but affectionately on the arm of her sister, 'is the penalty of experience, and, perhaps, the misfortunes of my nature ...' (176-77)

Her "misfortunes", as she herself sees them, begin with being the daughter of a woman of mixed blood. When the young colonel, Heyward, proposes to marry Colonel Munro's youngest daughter Alice, Munro says:

> 'There it was to my lot to form a connection with one who in time became my wife, and the mother of Cora. She was the daughter of a gentleman of those isles [West Indies], by a lady whose misfortune it was, if you will,' said the old man, proudly, 'to be descended, remotely, from that unfortunate class who are so basely enslaved to administer to the wants of a luxurious people.' (187-88)

The differences between the two sisters are emphasized throughout the novel: Cora is described as brunette: "[t]he tresses of this lady were shining and black, like the plumage of the raven. Her complexion was not brown, but it rather appeared charged with the colour of the rich blood, that seemed ready to burst its bounds" (21), while Alice has "golden hair which clustered about her brows; 'and yet her soul is as pure and spotless as her skin!' [says Cora]" (374). Due to her origin, says Geoffrey Rans in "Cooper's Leather-Stocking Novels", "[i]n romance terms, Cora is faced with death or dishonor; the dishonor refused, Magua is left only death to deal to satisfy his vengeance" (112). Living in the borderlands, belonging nowhere, feeling herself damned, Cora, the "woman with a cross", death is her only possible fate.

As Wasserman points out, Cora's cross "is part of the dramatization of the themes of separation and distinction central to a vision of the new land where the establishment requires that only one stance toward nature, one strand of history, one strain of the population impose themselves" (176). The mixed-blood girl, thus, although a very good, loyal and honest woman, is doomed for not being pure white, for, as Wasserman says, she "straddles the boundary that separates the white, civilized game from the nonwhite one" (175). She cannot be considered as one of the mothers of the nation, while her blonde sister certainly is. She dies and her love for Uncas, the Native American hero, cannot be fulfilled. Alice marries, and gives birth to several children who represent the future population of the US nation, a nation whose identity, for Cooper, is white.

Uncas, Cora's lover and a Mohican warrior, can be also situated as a liminal figure in the sense that, being in permanent contact with the white people, he has acquired certain white characteristics, which distinguish him from his fellowmen. As Wasserman states, Uncas can be seen as a counterpart to Natty, for the native is the closest to the boundary between whites and natives on the native side. He has his native manners changed, and he behaves as a chivalrous man toward the girls, showing that he is no longer a pure native in his moods and behavior:

> Uncas acted as attendant to the females, performing all the little offices within his power, with a mixture of dignity and anxious grace, that served to amuse Heyward, who well knew that it was an utter innovation on the Indian customs, which forbid their warriors to descend to any menial employment, especially in favour of their women. (65)

Uncas is doomed, however, not for having the cross of miscegenation, but because he dared to fall in love with a girl who, although not totally white, belongs to the other side of the boundary, to the white world of Cooper, in which interracial relations are totally denied. As Wasserman says, he is "doubly doomed, for not seeing the taint in her and for looking with desire across the line that separates them" (175).

Magua is another liminal figure in the novel. He is the villain who begins the texts as a guide and an interpreter, and he follows the pattern suggested by Hulme and which is discussed in the Introduction of this dissertation: liminal figures are not always trustworthy, and this is the case of the Huron man. Natty describes quite well the meaning of being a Huron:

> 'A Huron!' repeated the sturdy scout, once more shaking his head in open distrust; 'they are a thievish race, nor do I care by whom they are adopted; you can never make any thing of them but skulks and vagabonds. Since you trusted yourself to the care of one of that nation, I only wonder that you have not fallen in with more.' (65)

The fact that Magua uses different names is also an indication of his intentions towards his white companions; and, as his actual purposes are discovered, he runs away, instead of facing his enemies. He is the stereotype of the Bad Indian, who betrays the European and who has no good qualities at all. His conversation with Heyward clearly shows his character:

> The Indian riveted his glowing eyes on Heyward as he asked, in his imperfect English, 'Is he alone?'
> 'Alone!' hesitatingly answered Heyward, to whom deception was too new to be assumed without embarrassment. 'Oh! not alone, surely, Magua, for you know that we are with him.'
> 'Then le Renard Subtil will go,' returned the runner, coolly raising his little wallet from the

place where it had lain at his feet; 'and the pale faces will see none but their own colour.'
'Go! Whom call you le Renard?'
''Tis the name his Canada fathers have given to Magua,' returned the runner, with an air that manifested his pride at the distinction, though probably quite ignorant of the character conveyed by the appellation. 'Night is the same as day to le Subtil, when Munro waits for him.'
'And what account will le Renard give the chief of William Henry concerning his daughters? will he dare to tell the hot-blooded Scotsman that his children are left without a guide, though Magua promised to be one?'
'The gray head has a loud voice, and a long arm, but will le Renard hear him or feel him in the woods?' returned the wary runner. (48)

In *The Pioneers* (1823), besides Natty, who performs the same role, another liminal figure is the young Oliver Edwards / Effingham, who at fist presents himself as a mixed blood and who lives outside the town with Natty Bumppo and Chingachgook, another liminal figure in the novel. Oliver is torn between living in his friends' world and his own desire for revenge. By the end of the novel, when it is assured that he is not of mixed blood, he comes back to his place in the white world. But he is still in between, for he has lived with the natives long enough to consider himself one of them: "Cease to remember, old Mohegan, that I am the descendant of a Delaware chief, who once was master of these noble hills, these beautiful vales, and of this water, over which we tread"(197). Or, as Mr. Grant describes him:

> 'It is the hereditary violence of a native's passion, my child,' said Mr. Grant, in a low tone, to his affrighted daughter, who was clinging, in terror, to his arm. 'He is mixed with the blood of the Indians, you have heard; and neither the refinements of education, nor the advantages of our excellent liturgy, have been able entirely to eradicate the evil. But care and time will do much for him yet.' (136)

Cooper seems to be quite aware of de Pauw's ideas about racial degeneration caused by miscegenation, which I have discussed in Chapter 2. Although Mr. Grant cannot be seen as a reliable character, he is certainly exposing what were common ideas concerning the natives by the beginning of the nineteenth century. Yet, once it is known who Oliver really is, there is no evil in him anymore, and he can marry the white heroine Elizabeth, a marriage which otherwise would have been impossible in Cooper's universe.

Chingachgook, who in this novel is called John Mohegan or Indian John, assumes in this text the role of a liminal figure who lives neither in the white city nor in a Native American village. Instead, he lives, together with Natty and Oliver, in a hut near the woods. He is alone in the world, without family or progeny, and his death represents the end of his people, who may belong to the "immemorial past", without at least a chance of taking part in a "limitless future", as his last words indicate:

> 'Hawk-eye! my fathers call me to the happy hunting-grounds. The path is clear, and the eyes of Mohegan grow young. I look—but I see no white-skins; there are none to be seen but just and brave Indians. Farewell, Hawk-eye—you shall go with the Fire-eater and the Young Eagle, to the white man's heaven; but I go after my fathers. Let the bow, and tomakawk, and pipe, and the wampum, of Mohegan, be laid in his grave; for when he starts 'twill be in the night, like a warrior on a war-party, and he cannot stop to seek them.'(401)

His idea of a heaven without white skins would be a kind

of return to the past, to the moment before colonization, before contact in the Americas had been established, when being a Native American would not necessarily mean living on the border.

In Sedgwick's novel *Hope Leslie* (1827), the main cultural broker is Magawisca, who, from the very beginning is torn between her world and the white world represented by the Fletcher family. What Mrs. Fletcher says when the Native American girl arrives marks the difference between the two worlds:

> 'Magawisca,' she said in a friendly tone, 'you are welcome among us, girl.' Magawisca bowed her head. Mrs. Fletcher continued: 'you should receive it as a signal [of] mercy, child, that you have been taken from the midst of a savage people, and set in a Christian family.' Mrs. Fletcher paused for her auditor's assent, but the proposition was either unintelligible or unacceptable to Magawisca. (1:29)

Mrs. Fletcher's opinion, although not representing the narrative voice, is spread throughout the novel through the voices of some other characters, like Mrs. Hutchinson and the Reverend Mr. Cotton. Of course such an opinion is not shared by the native characters, but they do not have an expressive voice in the narrative. Nevertheless, Magawisca feels herself divided, split in two, for falling in love with Everell Fletcher and knowing that such a love is unacceptable by both her family and the boy's. When her father comes to kill Everell's mother and sisters, Magawisca is horrified. She

> uttered a cry of agony, and springing forward with her arms uplifted, as if deprecating his approach, she sunk down at her father's feet, and clasping her hands, 'save them--save them,' she cried, 'the mother—the children—oh they are all good—take vengeance on your enemies—but spare—spare our friends—our benefactors—I bleed when they are struck—oh command them to stop!' she screamed, looking to the companions of her father, who unchecked by her cries, were pressing on to their deadly work. (114-15)

To the end of the novel, Magawisca feels she does not belong anywhere.

Two other women play the same role, although with some differences: Nelema and Faith Leslie. The old

Native American woman lives by the woods near the white towns but keeps permanent contact with her own people. Like several women in her position, she is at one point accused of witchcraft, judged and condemned. Her intermediary position is clear from the very beginning, when Magawisca is still living with the Fletchers:

> She [Magawisca] did not doubt that Digby had really seen and heard him; and believing that her father shrink from a single armed man, she hoped against hope, that his sole object was to recover his children; hoped against hope, we say, for her reason told her, that if that were his only purpose, it might easily have been accomplished by the intervention of Nelema. (101-02)

Because she is not white and lives outside society, the moment she uses her medical knowledge she is accused of evil doings, just because her way of practicing medicine was not the same as that of the white men. As Susan Hill Lindley argues in *You Have Stept out of Your Place*, people who were accused of evil doings in New England were, first, overwhelmingly women, and mostly middle-aged or older, who "refused to accept the male authorities of church, state, and family and their own subordination thereto" (17-18), which is exactly Nelema's case, who, not belonging to white society, does not follow its rules. The white heroine, Hope Leslie, decides to help the old Native American woman exactly because Nelema mediates between the heroine and her sister Faith Leslie, who has been abducted as a child, as she says in a letter to Everell: "When she is gone, you will never again hear of Magawisca. I shall never hear more of my sweet sister. They both, if we may believe Nelema, still dwell safely in the wigwam of Mononotto, among the Mohawks" (1: 201).

Faith Leslie also lives in a contact zone, for she is white and married to a native American man. She feeds the worst Puritan fear: going native. Hope's reaction to her sister's marriage shows this fear: "'God forbid!' exclaimed Hope, shuddering as if a knife had been plunged in her bosom. 'My sister married to an Indian!'" (2: 31). The few moments, when Faith comes to her white family, she feels totally excluded, displaced:

> The poor girl obeyed, but without any apparent interest, and without even seeming conscious of the endearing tenderness with which Hope stroked back her hair, and kissed her cheek. 'What shall we do with this poor home-sick child?' she asked, appealing to her guardian.
> 'In truth, I know not,' he replied. 'All day, and all night, they tell me, she goes from window to window, like an imprisoned bird fluttering against the bars of its cage; and so wistfully she looks abroad, as if her heart went forth with the glance of her eye.' (2: 175)

Faith entered so far into the other's world that she cannot come back. No longer a white girl, but not yet a native, she has no place in the white world, and can only find one in the wilderness. As Slotkin points out, "the novel has a further message: it is possible for one to become wholly absorbed in the wilderness way of the Indian, to the extent that one loses all ties with the white world" (453). She is no longer a mediator or a liminal figure, once she sees herself as a native. However, from the point of view of the narrative, she could still be seen as a liminal figure.

Lydia Maria Child's *Hobomok* (1824) presents two

important liminal figures, Hobomok himself and the white girl he marries, Mary Conant. Several times Hobomok serves as a mediator between his white friends and other Native American people:

> In such a state of things, embassies and presents were frequently necessary to support the staggering friendship of the well disposed tribes. Accordingly, the second day after his arrival from Plymouth, Hobomok proceeded to Saugus, carrying presents from the English, and a message from Massasoit to Sagamore John. (54)

What makes Mary a liminal figure is her marriage to Hobomok, since the fact that she marries a Native American makes her different from everybody else in the town. Hobomok already lived outside Plymouth, and she goes to live there after their marriage. Thus, she becomes a very lonely person, isolated from everybody she knew. Not even her father accepts her marriage as a natural thing:

> 'She is married to Hobomok,' replied Mr. Skelton.
> The unexpected information fell like a deadly blow on the heart of the old man; and those

cheeks and lips grew pale, which no man had ever before seen blanched since his boyhood. He stood at the window a moment, firmly compressing his lips, to keep back some choking emotion; but finding the effort ineffectual, he took up his hat and went forth to seek a solitude where he might pour out his sorrows before his Maker.
(...)
'For her soul's salvation, God grant she may not be in her right mind,' answered Mr. Conant. 'I would fain have the poor stray lamb returned to the fold.' (241-42)

Considered mad by her family, she only recovers her status as a white person when Hobomok releases her from their marriage, and she goes back to her own place, where she finally marries the man she really loves. Her child, who would also become a liminal figure, as a mixed blood, has this fate prevented due to the fact that he is raised by his mother and his step-father. By the end of the novel it becomes clear that his native ancestry is to be forgotten, and seldom to be mentioned: "His father was seldom spoken of; and by degrees his Indian appellation was silently omitted" (198).

Almost all these liminal figures have, at one time or

another, carried out the work of interpreters and cultural brokers. Among them are the historical characters of Malinche, Paraguassú, and Pocahontas. Among the literary characters, Pocahontas, in the whole group of texts about her; Barclay and Namoutac, both in Custis's play; Natty Bumppo and Magua, in *The Last of the Mohicans* and *The Pioneers*; Magawisca, in *Hope Leslie*; and Hobomok, in Child's novel. But living on the border does not necessarily mean work as an interpreter; it more likely means living neither inside nor outside, but in between. The work of interpreter is carried out by liminal figures mostly because, due to their unique situation, they acquire great skill in language and communication. Likewise, these characters act as interpreters between white and Native American cultures, translating the language of each into terms the other can understand, and sometimes they must be selective in the meanings they choose to assign to their translations, in order not to be seen as traitors, like Magua, for he is not above distorting or even omitting the truth if he believes the circumstances warrant it.

I started this discussion with historical characters who were liminal figures for living in contact with two peoples and who carried out the work of interpreters and cultural brokers, as an attempt to show their importance to the construction of a national identity in their nations. Malinche, for instance, was a crucial figure in certain moments of Mexican colonization, when Cortez needed to make himself understood by the natives. And her son is considered the first "Mexican" boy, the one who represents the origin of his people, the Mexican people. Loved by many and hated by many others for having provided Mexico with this hybrid race, she is, as Anzaldúa says, not only "La Chingada" but also "La Madre", the mother of all Mexicans. Paraguassú, the Tupinambá girl, is also responsible for bringing into life a hybrid people, so mixed that it is impossible nowadays, in the Northeast of Brazil, to determine one's ascendance as pure. She has not acquired the mythological status given to Malinche, but she can certainly be seen as the mother of all Brazilians. Pocahontas, in the U.S.A., has a similar role, although with important and crucial differences: in Mexico and Brazil the colonizers (Spanish and Portuguese) considered miscegenation as one of the ways of conquering the land. Thus, the hybrid people of both countries, that may have had their origin in Malinche's and Paraguassú's children, soon became part of the colonized countries and, after their independence, part of the new nation[21]. In the U.S.A., however, as I have argued, miscegenation was not seen as natural or acceptable. So, Pocahontas is certainly the exception. Her son, who would also give origin to a hybrid people, was well accepted by white society, and did not have much trouble. Indeed, the fact that he was the son of an "Indian Princess" seems to have been very useful to him, for he married a wealthy white girl, from a traditional European family, and established Pocahontas's descendants as part of a Virginia aristocracy in such a way that even nowadays some Virginians claim to be her descendants.

Any of the literary characters discussed so far, besides the character of Pocahontas, were, in fact, as important as the historical characters in the matter of building a nation. However, they serve to illustrate how liminal figures were important at the beginning of the colonization and how their importance decreased as the new nation was taking form. Nevertheless, in any of the Pocahontas narratives it is not possible to deny her importance to the establishment of the first white settlement in Jamestown, the one that gave origin to Virginia, and, consequently, to the entire American nation. In the texts I have discussed, her role as mediator and cultural broker saved the lives of the white settlers more than once, and also helped establish peace between her people and the strangers, a peace that, historically, was settled by her marriage to the white colonist John Rolfe.

It is impossible to deny, after reading and analyzing some of the nineteenth century texts about Pocahontas, her importance as a cultural broker in the construction of the American nation and the establishment of an American national identity.

It is also impossible to deny that part of her actions as cultural broker and peacemaker happened because of her abduction by the white settlers, a subject that leads to the following aspect of the nineteenth century narratives about the Native American girl, which is the discussion of the captivity narratives inserted in these texts as well as in the novels of James Fenimore Cooper, Catherine Maria Sedgwick and Lydia Maria Child.

3.3. "Held as a hostage in the stranger's cell": Captivity Narratives in Romantic Texts on Pocahontas

Now see you here, I wear the clothes of an Englishwoman and will disturb you less when I walk. Here, I am Princess and Non Pareil of Virginia. I am Lady Rebecca. For me the Queen holds audience. Treachery, Captain, I was kidnapped!

Monique Mojica[22]

The child of Powhatan ye will not keep a prisoner? (...) Though alone, I am not defenseless. The Great Spirit's eye sleeps never, and His ear is never closed. Father and brother, ye shall find me true. From these I'll hide my grief; but once alone, I'll quench my fire in tears.

Charlotte Barnes[23]

During the post-revolutionary period, especially from 1800 to 1860, literary texts about white women captives and the "Indian Princess" Pocahontas were very common. Approximately forty texts were written about Pocahontas during this period, among novels, poems, plays and non-literary texts. Rebecca Blevins Faery states that these texts represent "the quest of the newly independent republic for a 'suitable' national history and identity, one that placed whiteness and masculinity in a superior position to other categories of identity" (15). Because Pocahontas was also a captive, it is important, in discussing the building of an American national identity, to see how the romantic texts about her deal with this subject. Besides, if the white captivity narratives placed whiteness and masculinity in a superior position, the Pocahontas narratives present a different perspective: although whiteness is also emphasized, it is through the female presence of the Native American girl that the captivity narrative develops. Because the central point of this dissertation is to show the importance of the Pocahontas narratives in the construction of an American national identity, it is not possible to deny that it was because of her captivity that Pocahontas met her future husband, was baptized, changed her entire life and promoted the so called "Peace of Pocahontas" by marrying a white colonist. It was during this peaceful period that the white settlers, feeling safer, could establish themselves in new lands and settle down in small farms and the first great tobacco plantations. When the natives arose against the white settlement of Jamestown, in 1622, the first British town in the Americas was no longer the only British settlement. The natives destroyed Jamestown, but the British were already well established in their colony and would never leave. It is quite probable that it would have happened even without the aid of Pocahontas, but this does not diminish her value as a peacemaker. As Tuomi Forrest argues, in "Maid to Order," Pocahontas's story represents the earliest example of *captivity-tale*, yet one opposite [to] what would become a familiar North-American genre. In the latter, the *White woman* recounted a story in which she was captured by the heathen Indians, but through her faith in God was restored to Colonial society, while the Indians received the divinely mandated and humanly enforced punishment. (3 – emphasis in the original)

Although the literary texts I analyze in this dissertation are all from 1800 to 1860, thus, from the post-revolutionary period, the first captivity narratives in the U.S.A., after Smith's ones, appeared by the end of the seventeenth century and were widely spread throughout the colonies till the end of the eighteenth century. Forrest refers to these first narratives, but the idea her text contains can be applied to later captivity narratives, including the fictional ones I deal with.

Considered by Richard Slotkin as the representative genre of the Anglo-American mode of contact with Native Americans, captivity narratives became popular during the seventeenth and eighteenth centuries, when true accounts of captives were published. These narratives, however, were written by whites, either male or female, who described the events in which they were involved during their captivity. None of the narratives published during this period told about the captivity of Native Americans, either male or female. Narratives of captive female natives were forgotten, and such women silenced, for they were not able to tell their stories. Such captives had their stories narrated by male European travelers who heard about them or who were eyewitnesses of their abduction. The text below, narrated by Michele de Cuneo (1495), Columbus's shipmate, describes how he and his men attacked a small party of Caribs, perhaps one of the first captivity narrative written in the Americas, in this case narrated by the captor instead of by the captive:

> We captured this canoe with all the men. One cannibal was wounded by a lance blow and thinking him dead we left him in the sea. Suddenly we saw him begin to swim away; therefore we caught him and with a long hook pulled him aboard where we cut off his head with an axe. We sent the other Cannibals together with the two slaves to Spain. When I was in the boat, I took a beautiful Cannibal

girl and the admiral gave her to me. Having her in my room and she being naked as is their custom, I began to want to amuse myself with her. Since I wanted to have my way with her and she was not willing, she worked me over so badly with her nails that I wished I had never begun. To get to the end of the story, seeing how things were going, I got a rope and tied her up so tightly that she made unheard of cries which you wouldn't have believed. At the end, we got along so well that, let me tell you, it seemed she had studied at a school for whores. The admiral named the cape on that island the cape of the Arrow for the man who was killed by the arrow. (Forrest 2)

This account of abduction and rape is of particular interest in relation to the Pocahontas narratives. Pocahontas too is abducted and treated as a coin of trade, but she has a different fate from the "Cannibal girl": because her father was considered as a great leader, and she achieved the status of a Native Princess, she was not ill-treated during her captivity, as Mossiker points out: "[a] daughter of the Supreme Chieftain of the tidewater could expected to be—and was—" very well, and kindly treated. (161). Afterwards, she was converted to Christianity, and, as Forrest argues, "[s]he has accepted

'Holy Faith', and thus was propelled away from 'whoredom' to 'sainthood' (5). Some of the historical cultural brokers discussed in this chapter are also part of such stories of Native American captives: Malinche is given by her mother from the Nahuatl people to a different people, the Chontal Maya, who finally give her to Cortez, and lives almost the rest of her life as a prisoner. Only her marriage to Juan Jaramillo somehow released her, and, like Pocahontas, she would never go back to her people. Like Pocahontas, she never told her own story, so that no one can know what she thought of the chain of events in which she was involved. One of Cortez's men, Bernal Díaz del Castillo, writes, in *The Discovery and Conquest of Mexico*, that she is an excellent woman, of obviously noble birth and bearing. He also describes her as "good looking and intelligent and without embarrassment" (2). The fact that she was given to the Chontal Maya before being given to Cortez provided her with a linguistic experience that was very useful to the Spanish conqueror, who used her services as an interpreter several times.

Malinche is many times compared to Pocahontas in the sense that both were forced to live with the strangers and served as interpreters of their culture and customs. As Bárbara González states in "Pocahontas and her Sister Malinche", "both women bravely confronted the other and gambled with love in order to save their people" (6). According to Gonzáles, Malinche won the gamble, since the Mexican people, no matter the name they call her, see her as their mother. Pocahontas, on the other hand, left only white descendants. However, she was so important to the establishment of the British colonies in the U.S.A. that her name is marked forever as the "mother" of all Americans, no matter their skin color.

It is important to notice that there is a great difference between female and male captivity narratives. While in the white female narratives there is always a hope that the captive's family will rescue her somehow, when the captive is a white male he needs a Native American maiden to rescue him.[24] Besides, the female captives, as Pauline Turner Strong points out, exemplify "the vulnerability of the Puritan colonies in New England" (132), for, as fearful daughters and/or mothers, the Puritan women are helpless before the native destroyers of their home, family and domestic order. As Strong argues, in captivity "all divinely sanctioned social roles are violated, accentuating the social disarray thought to be characteristic of the frontier." (132).

Mrs. Rowlandson's narrative (1682), for instance, describes a state of confrontation between the individual and the inferior other. Since she was a captive of the "heathens", the "inferior other" was controlling her. It was a condition that was outside her control. Her most important act was to pray — in communion with the "superior other" — and her release was eventually attributed to the compassion of the "superior other". Within this context, the "heathen", or "inferior other" represents wickedness just as the "superior other" represents the supreme good. The captive needs help from the "superior other" to prevail over the "inferior other". Both good and evil are states of the sublime. As Slotkin argues, "[h]er [Mrs. Rowlandson's] greater degree of natural sensibility and her experience as a captive made her more capable than her fellows of discovering and revealing the character of her soul, but the soul she revealed mirrored the aspirations and anxieties of Puritan America." (112).

Male captivities, on the other hand, present different representations of the white captive. Different from the females, who are given to different masters during their captivity, males are usually tortured and sometimes condemned to death. They are also taken through different native villages, exposed as trophies, and subjected to different kinds of humiliation. John Smith, for instance, posits himself at the center of his adventures, although narrating in the third person. He only needs the help of a young Native American girl to save him because of the extreme cruelty of her father:

> The Queene of Appamatuck was appointed to bring him water to wash his hands, and another brought him a bunch of feathers, in stead of a Towell to dry them: having feasted him after the best barbarous manner they could, a long consultation was held, but the conclusion was, two great stones were brought before Powhatan: then as many as could layd hands on him, dragged him to them, and thereon laid his head, and being ready with their clubs, to beate out his braines, Pocahontas the Kings dearest daughter, when no intreaty could prevaile, got his head in her armes, and laid her owne upon his to save him from death: whereat the Emperour was contented he should live to make him hatchets, and her bells, beads, and copper; for they thought him as well of all occupations as themselves. For the King himselfe will make his owne robes, shooes, bowes, arrowes, pots; plant, hunt, or doe any thing so well as the rest. (101)

Both John Smith's and Mrs. Rowlandson's texts can be seen as propaganda. Smith intends to describe the importance of the colonial enterprise so that he would be able to go back to Virginia, as William Gilmore Simms, in *Life of Captain Smith, the founder of Virginia*, says.

However, Simms states: "[i]f he could not go forth himself, he encouraged all who could do so" (372), using his writings with this objective. Mrs. Rowlandson published her ventures to promote the radical differences between the life of a truly Puritan woman and that of the "heathens". The former opened the doors to hundreds of texts about the "Indian Princess" who falls in love with the stranger and saves him at all costs; the latter allowed the beginning of a genre that becomes very popular during Romanticism, when several texts, mixing both kinds of captivity narratives, appear.

Besides Smith's and Rowlandson's narratives, another historical captivity narrative is Hannah Dustan's, narrated by Cotton Mather in *Magnalia Christi Americana* (1702). Although written long before Romanticism, this story is important because it reveals an opposite view to the Pocahontas's story. While in her captivity, Pocahontas was converted to Christianity, married a Christian man and was assimilated by white society; on the other hand, Hannah Dustan refuses to go into the alien world and kills her captors, inverting, for a moment, her role as a Puritan mother to revenge herself, being able to kill anybody, including a child, if it meant getting back to her own world. Mather included the story in a sermon like discourse with the objective of warning people against the temptations represented by Native Americans:

> But on April 30, while they were yet, it may be, about an hundred and fifty miles from the Indian town, a little before break of day, when the whole crew was in a dead sleep, (reader, see if it prove not so!) one of these women took up a resolution to imitate the action of *Jael* upon *Sisera*; and being where she had not her own life secured by any law unto her, she thought she was not forbidden by any law to take away the life of the murderers by whom her child had been butchered. She heartened the nurse and the youth to assist her in this enterprize; and all furnishing themselves with hatchets for the purpose, they struck such home blows upon the heads of their sleeping oppressors, that ere they could any of them struggle into any effectual resistance, '*at the feet of these poor prisoners, they bow'd, they fell, they lay down; at their feet they bow'd, they fell; where they bow'd, there they fell down dead.*' (634 – emphasis in the original)

Mather compares Dustan to one of the Biblical heroines, a woman who was God's instrument to release the Jews from twenty years of cruel oppression by Jabin the Canaanite and Sisera, his general. Thus, Jael killed Sisera and released the Jews (Judges 4:20-22). In comparing Hannah Dustan to Jael, Mather is using the Bible to support his own points: Mrs. Dustan is God's instrument to kill the Devil's offspring, the Puritans' enemies. It does not matter if she also kills children and women: they were all "savages", and "savages" were not to be respected. Besides comparing Hannah Dustan to Jael, Mather mentions another biblical passage which refers to the same episode, thus adapting it to fit his narrative: "At her feet he bowed, he fell, he lay; At her feet he bowed, he fell; Where he bowed, there he fell down dead" (Judges 26-28). His intention is clear: Mrs. Dustan, in releasing herself and the other prisoners, is releasing the chosen people, confirming in this way the Puritans' intentions to build a "city upon the hill"[25] in which Native American people could not be included. The violence perpetrated by Dustan against the Native Americans makes Leslie Fiedler consider hers the true anti-Pocahontas narrative, for while the Algonquian heroine presents a possibility of reconciliation between her people and the British, Dustan's narrative totally denies such a possibility.

Some of these historical captivities were, during the late eighteen century, fictionalized and transformed into literary texts, especially narratives concerning Pocahontas and John Smith. John Davis's text, *Travels of Four Years and a Half* (1803), portrays both male and female captivities, for in a first moment he tells how Smith was taken captive and rescued from death by Pocahontas, and afterwards he narrates her own abduction. This is how Davis narrates Smith's moment of execution:

> The next day a long and profound consultation was held by the King and his Privy Council, when a huge stone was brought before Powhatan, and several men assembled with clubs in their hands. The lamentations of the

women admonished Smith of his destiny; who being brought blindfolded to the spot, his head was laid on the block, and the men prepared with their clubs to beat out his brains. The women now became more bitter in their lamentations over the victim; but the savage Monarch was inexorable, and the executioners were lifting their arms to perform the office of death, when Pocahontas ran with mournful distraction to the stone, and getting the victim's head into her arms, laid her own upon it to receive the blow. Fair spirit! thou ministering angel at the throne of grace! if souls disengaged from their earthly bondage can witness from the bosom of eternal light what is passing here below, accept, sweet Seraph, this tribute to thy humanity.
Powhatan was not wanting in paternal feeling; his soul was devoted to his daughter Pocahontas; and so much did his ferocity relent at this display of innocent softness in a girl of fourteen, that he pronounced the prisoner's pardon, and dismissed the executioners. Indeed, every heart melted into tenderness at the scene. The joy of the successful mediator expressed itself in silence; she hung wildly on the neck of the reprieved victim, weeping with a violence that choked her utterance. (272-73)

It is possible to read this passage in different ways: first, Pocahontas's extreme goodness and sense of humanity contrast deeply with her father's and his men's behavior, a clear indication of her performance as a

"Good Indian", always willing to help the stranger, which later on takes her definitely to the white world. Then, it is also possible to see her role as a mediator between her father and the British soldier, as I have discussed in the previous part of this chapter, a role that allows her to save the stranger and to support the white settlement as a whole. She is said to have fallen in love with the man she saved, but he seems to be grateful, but not in love. The romantic pattern according to which the native maiden would save the stranger who then would marry her cannot be fulfilled.

In this, a male captivity narrative, there is no one to pay his ransom, and if it were not for the Native American girl he would have died. When she is the captive, however, the plot is a little different:

> In this critical situation of affairs, Captain Argall, who commanded one of the ships, devised an expedient to bring Powhatan to a compliance with their demands. His prolific brain was big with a stratagem, which, however unjustifiable, met with the concurrence of the Colonists. He knew the

affection which Powhatan bore for his daughter Pocahontas, and was determined to seize her.

Argall, having unloaded his vessel at the fort, sailed up the Potomac, under pretence of trading with the Indians who inhabited its banks. But he had been informed that Pocahontas was on a visit to Japazaws, King of Potomac, and his real motive was to gain over the savage by presents, and make him the instrument of putting Pocahontas into his power.

Japazaws had his price. For the promised reward of a copper-kettle, of which this savage had become enamoured, he prevailed on Pocahontas to accompany him and his Queen in a visit on board the ship; when Argall detained the betrayed girl, and conveyed her, with some corn he had purchased, in triumph to the fort. (288-89)

While Smith has been taken prisoner by Pocahontas's people when adventuring into the woods, Pocahontas was intentionally caught with the purpose of getting Powhatan's attention, so that the Algonquian chief would obey the colonists. While for a white female the idea of being a captive among the natives would be unbearable, for the native girl it seems to cause no great trouble. Contrary to her white counterparts, who, like Mrs.

Rowlandson, face their captivities as the ultimate nightmare, Pocahontas, at least in Davis's text, accepted her fate with tranquility, maybe joy. It was a good opportunity for her to be near her lover, who is no longer the man she saved. Smith had returned to England, injured in an accident, and asked his men to tell Pocahontas he was dead. Thus, while visiting his pretended grave, she meets John Rolfe, and they fall in love with each other. She, says Davis, "put herself under the protection of Rolfe who, by his tender, but respectful conduct, soothed her mind to tranquility" (289). Rolfe, who risked his life several times in trying to see her in her village, can now be with his lover without risk. While in Hamor's account, the first to describe her abduction, Powhatan takes too long to decide and ends up not paying any ransom, in Davis's novel the ransom is paid and Pocahontas released, just like many white captives, following in this case the same pattern: her family rescues her. However, she prefers to stay and marry Rolfe, which she eventually does.

In James Nelson Barker's text, *The Indian Princess* (1808), there is no mention of Pocahontas's abduction, since the play ends right after she has warned the British against a plot her father and the medicine man had planned against her white friends. Already a grown woman, she ends up engaged to John Rolfe, but not married yet. Smith's abduction, however, is well portrayed:

> WALTER. You shall hear. A league or two below this, we entered a charming stream, that seemed to glide through a fairy land of fertility. I must know more of this, said our captain. Await my return here. So bidding us moor the pinnace in a broad basin, where the Indian's arrows could reach us from neither side, away he went, alone in his boat, to explore the river to its head.
> LARRY. Gallant soul!
> WALTER. What devil prompted us to disobey his command I know not, but scarce was he out of sight, when we landed; and mark the end on't: up from their ambuscado started full three hundred black fiends, with a yell that might have appalled Lucifer, and whiz came a cloud of arrows about our ears. Three tall fellows of ours fell: Cassen, Emery, and Robinson. Our lieutenant, with Percy

and myself, fought our way to the water side, where, leaving our canoe as a trophy to the victors, we plunged in, and, after swimming, dodging, and diving like ducks, regained the pinnace that we had left like geese.
ALICE. Heaven be praised, you are safe; but our poor captain—
WALTER. Aye; the day passed and he returned not; we came back for a reinforcement, and to-morrow we find him, or perish. (128)

Although his friends decided to try to save him, he is instead rescued by the native girl, who risks her life to save him. Throughout the conversation concerning Smith's execution, the natives show two contrastive attitudes towards the prisoner: Nantaquas, Pocahontas's brother, as a representative of the "Good Indian" type, asks for Smith's life because he believes that the white man is his friend and has come "from a land beyond the wide water, to make [the native people] wise and happy!" (133); Miami and Grimosco, on the other hand, representing the "Bad Indian" type, demand Smith's death for believing he is of "a fearful race of beings" who "are not [their] god's children and who are "enemies to the Great Spirit" (132). Such a dichotomy, as it has been already discussed in Chapter 1, is very usual with Native Americans themes, the natives being either idealized, represented as "natural saints", or demonized, represented as "savage beasts". In captivity narratives the second type is prevalent, at least from the captive's point of view, who feels as if his/her own life has been dismantled, and he/she enters in an unknown world from which nothing really good can come. In John Smith's case, the rupture with civilization was not that violent, because he was already used to different adventures. And being saved by an "exotic princess" was not that unusual to him either[26]. In Barker's text, therefore, he is presented as a brave and fearless man, to whom death means nothing. In his discourse, he presents himself as a superior but merciful being who wants to help the inferior beings, the natives, to find their path to civilization:

> SMITH. Had not your people first beset me,

king,
I would have prov'd a friend and brother to them;
Arts I'd have taught, that should have made them gods,
And gifts would I have given to your people,
Richer than red men ever yet beheld.
Think not I fear to die. Lead to the block.
The soul of the white warrior shall shrink not.
Prepare the stake! amidst your fiercest tortures,
You'll find its fiery pains as nobly scorned,
As when the red man sings aloud his death-song.
(133 – my emphasis)

Smith talks about teaching, but not about learning. He proposes an asymmetrical relation, in which he and his men, for being white and "civilized" must teach the "uncivilized" red men. Barker portrays Pocahontas agreeing with him. She does not fall in love with Smith, but helps him anyway, accepting, from the beginning, the superiority, or, at least, understanding the enormous military power of the white people have over her own:

POCAHONTAS. Oh, do not, warriors, do not!

Father, incline your heart to mercy; *he will win your battles, he will vanquish your enemies*! [First signal.] Brother, speak! save your brother! Warriors, are you brave? preserve the brave man! (Second signal.] Miami, priest, sing the song of peace; ah! strike not, hold! mercy!

[Music. The third signal is struck, the hatchets are lifted up: when the PRINCESS, shrieking, runs distractedly to the block, and presses SMITH's head to her bosom.]

White man, thou shalt not die; or I will die with thee!

(133 – my emphasis)

George Washington Parke Custis's play, *Pocahontas, or The Settlers of Virginia* (1830), follows the same pattern; Smith's abduction is very well described; his rescue constitutes the climax, but there are no references to Pocahontas's abduction. In his conversation with Powhatan, Smith shows a total disrespect for the Algonquian leader and his customs. The English men subjugate the natives and Powhatan has no option but to accept a peace treaty with the stranger and the marriage of his daughter to the colonist John Rolfe.

Even before meeting Smith, Powhatan already fears him for he already heard of the adventurer's fame before meeting him:

> SELICTAZ: Great King! Smith! The leader Smith.— (Panting)
> POWHATAN: Well—Smith is not near Weorocomoco, I hope!
> SELICTAZ: Aye, great King, very near.
> POWHATAN: (Alarmed) Guards there! say quickly thy say—
> SELICTAZ: Smith is a prisoner, and will be here anon.
> POWHATAN: Ha! Prisoner! Smith a prisoner! And alive! Smith a prisoner!
> SELICTAZ: 'T is even so—Smith is thy prisoner, and alive.
> POWHATAN: Far beyond my hopes, thanks to the gods, and the brave Matacoran. (189)

Smith's discourse, in the following quote, shows how the captive considers himself superior to his captor, without even taking into account that Powhatan was the rightful leader of the whole Algonquian nation that, by the time the British reached American shores, occupied the coastal plain of Virginia from the south side of the James River north to the Rappahannock, for Powhatan had inherited the political control of six or seven tribes in the late sixteenth century, and then expanded his power through conquest to more than thirty tribes by 1607. Smith's words to Powhatan show his firm belief in his own superiority and in the superiority of his race over the others:

> SMITH: not a rusty nail would I give for ransom. I tell thee again, *old fool, 't is not thee but we are the conquerors in this fray*—that my banner, borne on the wings of victory, will soon be planted on thy throne—my war cry be heard in thy palace, and the royal James be sovereign of Virginia. (190)

Powhatan finally recognizes Smith's superiority, and admits he is inferior: "But experience makes *even* an Indian wise" (192 – my emphasis).

In spite of the strong eurocentric/ethnocentric discourse, Custis's play (1830) also presents a kind of reaction with the character Matacoran, Pocahontas's early suitor who is rejected when the girl meets John Rolfe. The young Native American warrior refuses the British man's friendship and, when Smith is rescued and affirms British superiority, he makes sure that he will be remembered as someone who "disdaining alliance with the usurpers of his country, nobly dar'd to be wild and free" (192). Matacoran is the only character in all the five narratives about her that does not quarrel with Smith and Rolfe because of Pocahontas's love, but mainly because he feels his people are in danger. Custis makes this Native American warrior foresee the future of his nation, and refuse to be part of it.

In Charlotte Barnes's play, *The Forest Princess* (1848), both Smith and Pocahontas's captivities are mentioned, and they happen in very similar ways. At first, Smith goes to Weorocomoco by his own will to present himself and to announce that his king intends to conquer the land. When Powhatan refuses to accept his proposal of peace, considering it dangerous to his people, Smith threatens the Algonquian chief with the British army. He is totally fearless before death, and treats Powhatan as an inferior, in cultural terms:

> Powhatan: Powhatan will no treaty make - no peace –
> The pale-faced brethren come to spy - to seize
> His lands - to make his tribes their slaves - to bow
> Him down with tribute.
> SMITH: Chief, you wrong me much,
> And wrong still more your father, England's king.
> Ambition, avarice, may be the curse
> Of some who sought your friendship to betray.
> My word is sacred as my bond. In deeds,
> As well as speech, I proffer amity.
> (...)
> SMITH: Yet hear me, savage chief!
> POWHATAN: Plead not! 't is vain.
> SMITH: Plead! 't is for thyself
> I'd speak. 'Beware the vengeance of my king.
> Plead! never! Death I fear not. I will meet
> Its stroke with firmness as a soldier should.
> My peace I trust is made above. My life,
> Risked for my country oft, is England's still. (332)

At least in this text, Powhatan is conscious of what may happen to him and to his people if white people conquer his land. Smith, on the contrary, is Eurocentric, without the least concern for what the Algonquian chief thinks. He even calls the Native American leader "savage", a word which carries a very pejorative sense. Smith is presented as a great leader, someone able to control his emotions and who does not fear death if it is for the good of his country. Barnes has Smith and Powhatan facing one another with dignity and respect, although she makes clear, in the speeches of both leaders, that the relationship between their people cannot be a relationship of equals. In calling Powhatan a "savage", Smith is saying that he himself is civilized, establishing, then, a very asymmetrical relationship that has been the pattern in these texts.

In Barnes's narrative, Pocahontas's captivity is similar to Smith's in the sense that she has also come to the white settlement by her own will in order to warn the colonists against Volday's plot, unlike what happens in the narratives of Custis and Barker. Once in the settlement, she is not allowed to leave, so that Powhatan would be forced to accept the peace proposal. She reacts first with anger, than with fear. Were it not for John Rolfe she would certainly have despaired. However well treated, she felt her imprisonment on the white village as an insult to her dignity as a Native American princess as well as an act of treachery for all she had already done to help them:

> RATLIFFE: You pass not here young girl.
> POCAHONTAS: (With dignity) I am a warrior's daughter, and am called Virginia's princess. Stranger, stand aside.
> DALE: All courtesy we'll show thee, lady, but thy father's peace and friendship we would gain by this one act. (He gives a signal and each entrance is guarded)
> POCAHONTAS: The child of Powhatan ye will not keep a prisoner?
> DALE: But until her father signs a peace. (Pocahontas starts but instantly recollects herself) You deem this strange? Policy demands this step.
> POCAHONTAS: No policy doth Pocahontas know, save justice. She hath succored ye, for she believed ye friends. But if your arms should ever be leveled against her race, mark well! Her country's foes are hers. (342)

This is the only moment in all these texts on Pocahontas in which she rebels against the stranger's will, the only moment in which her love for her people is stronger than her love for the white man she is to marry. After all, she was betrayed when she was trying to help, and, as the text makes clear, ingratitude is something hard to stand. Before being released, when the messenger has just been sent to her father, she criticizes the white men for doing exactly what they condemn in Native American behavior:

> POCAHONTAS: In a daughter's ear,
> who dares to breathe that word against her sire?
> To free his country from invaders' tread
> He tries the arts his rugged life has taught.
> Ye blame the red man, yet adopt his wiles.
> Why do ye practice treachery, deceit,
> Trampling on hospitable gratitude
> By thus constraining me? Oh shame! The stream
> Of patriot love flows in my father's heart,
> Though shadowed so by dark enlacing woods,
> The Sun of mercy cannot always pierce
> Their thick unwholesome gloom. No such excuse
> Is yours; for from the current of your souls
> The Tomahawk of Ages has been hewn down

> All that impeded the pure light of heaven! (343)

All the texts I am dealing with were written during Romanticism, and all then present Pocahontas as fighting against her father for the stranger's sake, a pattern that is used during Romanticism but that has its origin long before. In Barnes's text, however, Pocahontas tries to react against her abduction, a reaction that is not seen in any of the other texts. In making the native girl react against the strangers' acts, Barnes reinforces the idea that her marriage to John Rolfe was not a political or economical arrangement, but a true love relationship, for, although angry with the white leaders, she could not deny her love for the British planter.

In Lydia Sigourney's poem "Pocahontas", both Smith's and Pocahontas's captivities are mentioned. In this text, Smith is not as arrogant as he is in the previous ones. Powhatan, nevertheless, fears the enemy's power; hence his decision to kill Smith before white people could dominate his land:

> But he, that wily monarch, stern and old,
> Mid his grim chiefs, with barbarous trappings bright,
> That morn a court of savage state did hold.
> The sentenced captive see — his brow how white!
> Stretch'd on the turf his manly form lies low,
> The war-club poises for its fatal blow,
> The death-mist swims before his darken'd sight:
> Forth springs the child, in tearful pity bold,
> Her head on his declines, her arms his neck enfold. (XVIII)

Contrary to Powhatan, who fears the white people, Pocahontas, in this poem, is eager to join them. Thus, her captivity is not a hardship, for she and Rolfe have fallen in love and want to stay together. She accepts the Christian faith, and is baptized, refusing to go back to the wilderness:

> On sped the tardy seasons. Need I say
> What still the indignant lyre declines to tell?
> How, by rude hands, the maiden, borne away,
> Was forced amid the invaders' homes to dwell?
> Yet no harsh bonds the guiltless prisoner wore,
> No sharp constraint her gentle spirit bore,
> Held as a hostage in the stranger's cell;

> So, to her wayward fate submissive still,
> She meekly bow'd her heart to learn a Saviour's will. (XXIX)

In all cases, when these texts about Pocahontas deal with her abduction, it is clear that the native woman is not supposed to go back to her people, her customs, and her traditions. She will stay with the strangers, accept their religion, and marry one of them. Although she is abducted and forced to stay with the alien people, all these texts present Pocahontas as accepting to live with the British without much hesitation. According to the authors, love is what moves the native girl. So, the moment she falls in love either with John Smith (in John Davis's novel) or with John Rolfe (in the five texts I have discussed), she has her fate traced: she will always choose to be with her white lover, no matter how. Pocahontas is not passive or submissive, though. On the contrary, she is portrayed, in the five texts I have discussed, as someone who has her own life in her hands, and who acts acording to her own will, except when she is abducted. In the texts in which her abduction is mentioned, she is released but refuses to go back to her people, for the man she loves would not be there.

A very important character in all these texts about Pocahontas is her father, Powhatan, who has a very contradictory behavior: he is portrayed as cruel and merciless towards his enemies, but seems to have very "tender emotions" in relation to his daughter. And it is this last feeling that prevails, for he ends up, in all the five narratives, accepting to spare Smith's life and Pocahontas marriage to John Rolfe. He is neither totally incorporated in the "Bad Indian" type, the worst denomination the natives could have from the European point of view, nor in the "Good Indian" type, the best description a native would have still according to the Europeans. In the first case, to be a "Bad Indian" means to be really bad, without any kind of mercy, no matter the others' feelings. If he were portrayed as a true "Bad Indian", Smith and his men would have died in the texts, which would not be accepted by the readers, since the texts are adaptations of a real story. If he were portrayed as a true "Good Indian", the climax of the narratives, which is Smith's life being saved by Pocahontas, would not have occurred, which would also be unacceptable. Thus, Powhatan is portrayed as someone moved by the emotions of the moment, either anger, in relation to the British, or love, in relation to his daughter. This portrayal of Powhatan is not new. John Smith, in *Generall Historie* (1624), also gives this contradictory view about the Native American leader.

Besides the Pocahontas narratives, other romantic texts deal with captivity narratives in a different way. While in the Pocahontas narratives she is abducted for political and economical reasons, and does not have her life threatened, the other narratives portray the abductions as moved by a war situation in which the characters are involved, as in James Fenimore Cooper's *The Last of the Mohicans* (1626), or moved by a desire of revenge, as in Catherine Maria Sedwick *Hope Leslie* (1627). In Cooper's

The Last of the Mohicans, Cora, the mixed blood girl, is taken captive by the villain, Magua, and is killed while the young Mohican, Uncas, tries to rescue her. He is also murdered. A happy ending is not possible because of her mixed blood and Uncas's race, such a narrative does not really follow the pattern of white women captivity narratives, first because Cora is not really "pure white", and also because her intended savior is not white either, but a Native American. This leads to the conclusion that they would never be together in Cooper's world, a world in which miscegenation is not allowed. In Catherine Maria Sedwick's novel, *Hope Leslie*, however, such a union between two people of different races can be accepted once they live outside the white society. As Richard Slotkin argues, Sedgwick "violates Puritan psychology" for asserting that Faith's "proper place is now with her Indian husband and in seeing this acculturation in a positive light, rather than a sort of degeneracy" (453). It is Magawisca who clarifies this to

Hope Leslie:

> 'Both virtue and duty,' [Magawisca] said, 'bind your sister to Oneco. She hath been married according to our simple modes, and persuaded by a Romish father, as she came from Christian blood, to observe the rites of their law. When she flies from you, as she will, mourn not over her, Hope Leslie — the wild flower would perish in your gardens — the forest is like a native home to her — and she will sing as gaily again as the bird that hath found its mate.' (214)

As the passage shows, Faith has also married according to Christian laws, although not Puritan. Thus, she has not only gone native, but also converted to Catholicism, two great fears the Puritans had. However, it is by means of captivity that the characters of *Hope Leslie* have found their proper place in the world, their proper social setting. The social world of Puritan Christendom is clearly suitable for Everell and Hope, while for Faith and Oneco the appropriate world is that of the wilderness. As Slotkin declares, "captivity is the means for whatever acculturation the whites are permitted to undergo, the means of whatever reconciliation between Indian and settlers is possible" (454). This may be true in relation to Pocahontas and Faith Leslie, whose captivities end up with their total acculturation. However, this is not true in relation to Cora Munro, who dies, or to Hannah Dustan, who kills her captors in a violent way. Comparing the texts of Cooper, Sedgwick and Child with those about Pocahontas, one sees that captivity narratives are marked by extremely asymmetrical relations of power, in which the stronger group cause pain and suffering to the captive. This happens from both sides, European and Native American. In the texts on Pocahontas, for instance, Powhatan is portrayed as evil and cruel only at the moment of executing Smith. After he decides to release the prisoner, his attitude changes as he incorporates the stranger into the community, showing, thus, that there is no need to prove his superiority through violence. Things are not different when Pocahontas is abducted, white power does not allow her to go back home, although there is no real threat against her life in any of the texts. After her marriage to John Rolfe, she is not a prisoner any more, and thus their treatment of her changes, as she is free to come and go as she wishes. In all the texts, no one dares to touch her physically. This does not happen in the other texts where captivity occurs, such as Cooper's *The Last of the Mohicans*, in which Cora is murdered for refusing to marry her captor. Although Magua can be considered an "inferior other" in relation to Cora, who is civilized, he detains the power of death and life upon her while she is his captive. There is a sense in which, once inserted in a captivity, no matter the values of each culture, the captive becomes the subjugated one and has either to accept his / her fate or die. Pocahontas is the only exception, because of her important deeds before the abduction, and also because of her status, never forgotten by the romantic writers, as an "Indian Princess".

In *Hope Leslie* (1626), for instance, Magawisca's older brother, a sixteenth-year-old boy, is killed by British soldiers for refusing to betray his father, while in captivity, which makes her father angry and desirous of revenge. She herself is taken captive, and forced to live with a Puritan family to whom she is uncivilized and savage. Her family, following the pattern when the captive is a woman, although in this case a native one, rescues her at a high cost for the white family. But violence happens either if the captive is a Native American or a white person, as the firsthand captivity narratives certainly assure: in all of them, with the exception of Hannah Dustan's narrative, there are extremely violent acts against the captives. Captivity represented, to the Puritans, an allegorical struggle of good against evil, or an opportunity for martyrdom. The experience of captivity gives to the captive a sense of dependency, lack of control, a vulnerability to being either completely isolated or never left alone. Captives were forced into an often brief but total assimilation of the stranger's ways, which in some cases proves to be positive, as in Faith Leslie's or Pocahontas's case, whose captivities lasted as long as they lived for having married one of the strangers. But, depending on the point of view, only Pocahontas's crossing was positive, for Faith Leslie entered in a "dark world" from which she would not be able to escape, the world without a "true" religion. However, Faith, once restored to her white relatives, proves to be as uncivilized as a native. She and her Native American husband finally succeed in escaping to the wilderness, the only interracial couple in a frontier romance to achieve a happy ending.

The captivity narratives had a strong influence upon the colonies and on the Native American nations. Whatever their failures in assimilating people of different beliefs and customs, the British colonies, like other European outposts throughout the Americas, were too big and aggressive for the natives to ignore even if they wanted to. Throughout the seventeenth and eighteenth centuries the English presence was sharply imposed on the natives; diseases and wars dramatically reduced their numbers; wars in which several captives were taken from both sides, land sales, migrations, and missionary endeavors drastically changed their settlement patterns; technological innovations permanently altered Native Americans' economic and occupational customs; and Christian teachers and missionaries made major incursions into the natives' fundamental modes of communication and belief. Native American societies had never been stagnant, but not until the seventeenth and eighteenth centuries did they undergo such a cultural revolution. Native American life would never be the same.

Neither would Euro-American life. The early settlers' intention to transplant the best of European culture and to remain aloof from Native American "barbarity" proved useless. From the very beginning Native American culture exerted a subtle but deep influence on the newcomers: in language, travel, warfare, food, clothing, entertainment, and many other aspects of American life. And the captivity narratives had an important role in such an influence, as they were published and spread throughout the country. They served as reference to the natives' ways of living, their daily life and their traditions, so that the readers would learn and fear. As Dorsan says, the captivity narratives "illustrate Indian behavior in ways apparent only to the day-by-day and inside observer. Carved pure out of the American scene, they make real indeed a frightful and ever present danger to which the pioneer settlers were exposed" (170).

From this analysis it is possible to conclude that both historical and literary captivity narratives were important to the construction of a national identity at the beginning of the nineteenth century. The historical ones because they helped establish the kind of boundary between whites and Native Americans, a boundary marked basically by cultural differences. And the literary ones because they reinforce and/or question this boundary, the line that is impossible to cross in James Fenimore Cooper's novels but that is crossable both in the texts about Pocahontas and in the novels by Lydia Maria Child and Catherine Maria Sedgwick. Living among alien people, as a captive, allowed Pocahontas, in the five narratives about her, to meet the man she loves, and to decide her fate as a mediator figure. Hers is, either historically or literally, a remarkable crossing, the first native girl to accept the Christian faith and to marry a white colonist in the land that would become the U.S.A., a crossing that is not frequently imitated, so that it is considered an important event in American history.

Contrary to Pocahontas and Faith Leslie, and the historical Malinche before them, whose captivities end with their marriage and their complete assimilation into the others' world, the other narratives discussed in this dissertation show a strong resistance from the captives' part to identify themselves with their captors. John Smith, for instance, repeats, in all the texts, that he is a soldier ready to die for his country, never to be subjected to his captors. Mrs. Rowlandson, whose narrative is considered by some writers, like Richard Slotkin, as an archetype of the genre within American culture (94), describes, in her narrative, the efforts she makes to keep herself apart from the natives' customs. And Cora Munro, the "woman with a cross" in Cooper's novel *The Last of the Mohicans*, prefers to die than to marry her captor Magua. Of course Cora, unlike Smith and Rowlandson, is totally fictional, but her behavior towards the natives and her attitude in relation to her captor serve to illustrate the proper behavior of a Christian girl under such circumstances. The possibility of "becoming natives" was so frightening; at the same time it was so close to the captives, that the only way the captives had to avoid it was keeping themselves in isolation. These narratives strongly influenced the construction of an American national identity at the beginning of the nineteenth century, when American writers were narrating their new nation, for they helped, to a certain point, to establish the place the natives should occupy, given the threat they represent to the "civilized" people. Thus, with the exception of Pocahontas, the other natives included in the narratives I have discussed are not supposed to be part of the present-day American nation. Nobody can deny that the natives belong to the glorious past of the American Nation, but they are to remain in the past.

As I have said at the end of the previous chapter, the three aspects discussed in this chapter are closely related. The issue of miscegenation, so feared in James Fenimore Cooper's novels, appears in the Pocahontas narratives as a possibility of assimilating the natives into the white world. This possibility, in the narratives, becomes stronger as Pocahontas is kidnapped and forced to live with the strangers. If before the abduction she is already a mediating figure, after living a while with the British her role as a liminal figure becomes more evident. The same happens to Magawisca, the young native girl of Catharine

Maria Sedgwick in *Hope Leslie*: forced to live with her people's enemies, she tries to mediate between her father and the white family she lives with. She fails in saving some of the white people's lives, but she does not fail in saving her lover's life. Living at the woods with her family, the girls still acts as a mediating figure, bringing news from Faith Leslie, who is abducted as a child and lives with the natives. It was her abduction that allowed her to learn the English language and to become a mediating figure. It was also through abduction that Pocahontas could meet John Rolfe and marry him, bringing a hybrid race to the world. Thus, it is impossible to dissociate the three aspects and necessary to understand the importance of such aspects in the construction of an American national identity. Traditionally, American identity is related to the Puritans, as Scavan Bercovitch says in *The Puritan Origin of an American Self*. However, through the analysis of these narratives it is possible to notice that the natives are also part of this identity, even if in a subtle way. Otherwise, why would Pocahontas's story be so widely re-narrated? And why would Cooper fear so much the miscegenation? Not thinking of giving a definite answer, but trying to give one possible answer, I would say that the fear of miscegenation comes from the close relationship established between the white settlers and the Native American people during the colonization process. The close relationship, sometimes forced through abductions in war times, brings the fear of mixing the races so that both people would slowly disappear, and a new hybrid race would come into being. Pocahontas's story is an example of such a possibility, an example that is not followed, so that white supremacy prevails. But the number of texts about Pocahontas and other natives at the moment the new nation was narrating itself is very significant. At the same time Cooper published his Leather-stocking series, American theaters were presenting a series of plays with native themes, portraying a world that, different from Cooper's world, raises a possibility of assimilating the natives without necessarily killing them. This way the natives would belong not only to the past, but also to the present and the future of the nation.

CONCLUSION

And so here ends the legend of the Princess Pocahontas-
Fa la la la lay, fa la la la la LELF-
   if you want any more, make it up yourself.
               Monique Mojica[1]

History is history. You're not honoring a nation of people when you change their history.
               Custalow-MacGowan[2]

Come, and go, like Pocahontas
Leaving but a glow to haunt us
For a love the soul remembers
Dreaming by December's embers.
               Hervey Allen[3]

I have tried to show that the Pocahontas narratives have been part of the construction of an American national identity during the first half of the nineteenth century, a period some writers like Sacvan Bercovitch and Myra Jehlen call "the American Renaissance" or "American Romanticism". I have also established a relation between the Pocahontas narratives and two novels of James Fenimore Cooper, *The Last of the Mohicans* (1826) and *The Pioneers* (1823), as well as between the same narratives and the novels of Catherine Maria Sedgwick, *Hope Leslie* (1827), and Lydia Maria Child, *Hobomok* (1824).

The relation between these narratives arises through the ways in which they deal with the anxieties and conflicts between whites and Native Americans, especially with the possibility of miscegenation and its consequences. This relation also appears when one takes into consideration the different ways in which female and male centered texts deal with the theme of miscegenation, as well as with captivities. I have tried to show that both miscegenation and captivity narratives acquire different connotations depending on the captive's race and gender. I have also discussed both in male and female centered texts, how these texts, in dealing with the anxieties and conflicts between whites and Native Americans, approach the presence of different liminal figures, whose portrayals greatly differ according to their gender and race.

If nations are historical constructs, then all the texts mentioned above construct and narrate different nations. However, there are also some similarities in their constructions and narrations. In the Pocahontas narratives, for instance, the nation that is "imagined" by the writers, to use Benedict Anderson's terminology, is one in which cultural conflicts between Native Americans and British settlers were not serious enough to impede miscegenation and the consequent assimilation of the cultures to each other.

Such cultural conflicts were caused especially by

anxiety arising from the awareness both people had of their differences; yet, they could also ignore the others' culture and customs, or even consider these customs as inferior to their own, as the use of words like "savage" indicates. However problematic, the relationship between the natives and the white settlers in the narratives about Pocahontas is not seen as forbidden or unnatural, but as a way of assimilating the natives into the white world. Nevertheless, because these narratives were written by white writers, the natives were idealized, as part of the Romantic ideology of that period, which makes the assimilation of the natives into the white world totally fictional, hers being an exception.

In John Davis's text, *Travels of Four Years and a Half in the United States of America* (1803), for instance, although he portrays a single interracial marriage, the union is approved by both natives and whites, reinforcing a close relationship between the two people and allowing the possibility of other interracial relationship, although none is mentioned in the text. There is no mention of miscegenation as an actual problem for the people involved. Indeed, although the discourse is Eurocentric, and the British people are seen as culturally, politically and socially superior, there is no mention of racial issues. The fear of miscegenation, as Robert Tilton suggests, may be present to a certain point, but is not strong in the Pocahontas narratives. The emphasis on Smith's rescue is probably due to the fact that this event is important not only to Virginia or Virginian aristocracy to which her marriage is related, but also to the construction of an American nation.

In the texts in which Pocahontas does not marry John Rolfe, James Nelson Barker's *The Indian Princess* (1808) and George Washington Parke Custis's *Pocahontas* (1830), miscegenation is not portrayed as a great problem either. In Barker's text, for instance, the play ends with the possibility of two interracial marriages in a near future: Pocahontas and John Rolfe, Nima and

Robin. And the concern the characters have about such unions is due to their cultural differences, the same happening in Custis's text in which there is already a couple of mixed ancestry: Mantea is a Native American woman, and Barclay is a British settler, but they do not face any trouble for being together. The cultural differences are not perceived as causing any serious trouble. Although these texts also present a Eurocentric view, they open the possibility of an assimilation that would build a different nation.

Charlotte Barnes's *The Forest Princess* (1848) and Lydia Sigourney's poem "Pocahontas" (1841), also deal with the possibility of a nation in which the natives are to be assimilated. In both texts Pocahontas's marriage to John Rolfe and the birth of their son are well received, and racial differences are not taken into consideration either. As for cultural differences, both peoples seem to be ready to overcome them as peace is achieved, so that it would not really represent a problem. In these narration of their new born nation, the authors find a place for the natives in their world through assimilation, so that they would belong both to the past and to the present with a place in the future as well.

However, while presenting their narration of the new American nation, in none of the Pocahontas narratives, the authors do a clear reference to the violence natives and whites perpetrated against each other. This shows the need to forget some difficult things, such as the violence and cruelty one people practiced against the other, at the beginning of colonization, and to remember only the good things, such as the events that gave birth to Thanksgiving Day. By forgetting the violence that generated the nation, the authors of these narratives about Pocahontas open the way to a narrative of the nation that emphasizes white supremacy, but does not deny the possibility of including the natives in this narrative. These narratives also determine that, in order for the natives to enter the new nation, they would have to behave as the

"Good Indian" type, always willing to help the white people to assure their superiority. The natives who would behave as the "Bad Indian" type would be totally lost for the new nation, as Matacoran's fate, in Custis's *Pocahontas* (1830), indicates.

While the Pocahontas narratives open the possibility of natives' assimilation, the so-called founding narratives of James Fenimore Cooper totally deny such a possibility. The nation "imagined" by Cooper is white, Anglo-Saxon, Protestant. In his novels, there are no options for any other kind of people, especially mixed-blood people. The fate of the important native characters in the two narratives I discussed in Chapter 3 is an indication of such a narrative of the American nation: Uncas, the last descendant of the great Mohicans, dies; his father, Chingachgook, the last of his people after his son's death, also dies; Magua is the "Bad Indian" of the narrative and also dies. Thus, there are no natives left to take part in the nation Cooper narrates.

For Cooper, the natives belong neither to the present nor to the "immemorial past", for, in his point of view, such a past does not exist. As Renata Wasserman points out, Cooper believes that American history begins with the arrival of the Europeans, creating a kind of "psychological time", a time that is "measured in actions rather than in eons" (181). Wasserman states that

> Emphasis and attention to detail make American history seem as long as European history, the founders as long-lived as biblical patriarchs, their peopling and civilizing of the New World as weighty as the birth of European nations. He is careful not to extend these "mists of time" beyond the moment in which colonization started, however, for the other premise of his account is that the European colonizers created the New World out of nothing. (181)

This way, the only place the natives would have in Cooper's world is the place a vanishing people should have, that is, no place at all. However, since the natives are to vanish, the whites, in order better to survive in the American wilderness, must learn how to live like a native without becoming one. Thus, the extreme concern of

Natty Bumppo, the protagonist of both *The Last of the Mohicans* and *The Pioneers*, to assure all, at all times, that he is a "man without a cross" (*The Last of the Mohicans* 80), even if he behaves like a native in hunting and warfare. In *The Last of the Race: The Growth of a Myth from Milton to Darwin*, Fiona J. Stafford emphasizes Cooper's need to situate his hero as belonging to "a stronger race" (233) a pronounced idea in *The Last of the Mohicans*. To Stafford, there is, in Cooper's novel "a strong undercurrent of relief in the assertion that the natives could no longer pose a threat" (233).

Like the captives portrayed in the captivity narratives, Natty keeps himself almost in isolation, in order to make sure he will never become a native. In his narration of the American nation, Cooper does mention the natives' violence against whites, but not the other way around. Because the natives may not be part of the American nation, forgetting the violence against them but remembering how violent they are makes it easier to exclude them from the nation. As Cooper himself states, in *Notions of the Americans* (1828), "the red man disappears before the superior moral and physical influence of the white" (368), an idea that he emphasized throughout his novels.

It is possible to say that the Pocahontas narratives present an opposite view of the American nation when compared with Cooper's novels: the texts about Pocahontas allow the possibility of miscegenation, Cooper's novels do not; in the Pocahontas narratives the nation has an "immemorial past", a mythical past long before the arrival of the European, Cooper's American nation can only begin with the arrival of the Europeans; the female captive in the texts about Pocahontas is to be incorporated into the other's world through marriage, she is to die in Cooper's text, or to be rescued before any damage to her personality is done, as it happens to Alice Munro, so that interracial marriage may never occur; Pocahontas's story presents her as an important mediating figure able to bring peace between her people and the whites, in Cooper's novel such an important female figure does not exist. Thus, the nation imagined by the authors of these contrasting narratives is totally different, although they are narrating the way they understand the same nation. This shows that a single national identity is not possible, for there are different possibilities.

One of these other possibilities is presented by Catherine Maria Sedgwick's *Hope Leslie* (1827) and Lydia Maria Child's *Hobomok* (1824). These two narratives present a view of the American nation intermediary between that of the Pocahontas narrative and of Cooper's novels. They allow miscegenation, but it must not happen in the white settlements. Captivity, with all the terrors it may bring, includes a positive aspect, for it is through captivity that both Faith Leslie and Magawisca find their destiny and the men they love. Magawisca renounces her love when she understands that he would never live in the wilderness with her since he is white, and she, as an important figure in her nation, could not live in the white world. Faith, on the other hand, marries Oneco and both live happily ever after in the natives' world. In *Hobomok* (1824), the mixed couple cannot keep their marriage because they live close to the white society, so their relationship ends. In narrating the nation, both Sedgwick and Child mention violent acts from both sides. In this way, these narratives do not totally exclude the natives, although portraying assimilation as the only way they could belong to the nation.

The idea of the natives as vanishing people and part of the immemorial past of the American nation is also present in these narratives of the American nation. Both mention the possibility of interracial marriage between native women and white men, in which case the couple would be able to live in white society, and assimilation would be possible. As has been shown, white women are not supposed to marry outside the white world, unless they totally renounce their customs and traditions, as Faith

Leslie does. Native women, on the other hand, would assimilate to white customs, and their mixed blood children would be raised according to white customs, as in the narratives about Pocahontas. When a white woman marries a native and does not move to the wilderness, such a union cannot last, as in Mary Conan's marriage in *Hobomok* (1824).

The nation imagined by both *Hope Leslie* (1827) and *Hobomok* (1824) is similar to the one imagined in the Pocahontas narratives, with some important differences: in the Pocahontas narratives, although some of the mixed blood couples, like Mantea and Barclay in Custis' play, *Pocahontas or the Settlers of Virginia* (1830), or Pocahontas and John Rolfe in Davis's *Travels* (1803), live outside the villages, they do not need to go to the wilderness as in the narratives of Sedgwick and Child because both females are native, so they can be assimilated by the white world; in the texts about Pocahontas few scenes of violence of one people against the other are present, while in Sedgwick's narrative the violence is part of the nation's past. However, some important similarities can also be perceived among these different narratives: these texts present assimilation as a possibility in the building of the new nation, and they also present important female mediating figures like Pocahontas and Magawisca, who were able to defy their fathers in order to establish, or at least fight for, peace.

In short, Cooper's narratives are the ones that present the Puritan view of the American nation pointed out by Sacvan Bercovitch in which there is no place for non white people. Copper presents an exclusivist white nation while the Pocahontas narratives and the novels of Sedgwick and Child present a nation in which there is the possibility of inclusion.

The texts analyzed give totally different views of an "imagined community". Some of them, like the Pocahontas narratives, portray Native Americans as part of the "immemorial past" but with a limited role in the "limitless future", unless they are assimilated into the white world through marriage. This is the same view presented by the texts of Sedgwick and Child, while for Cooper the natives have no place at all. There seems to be not a single American identity, Puritan or Pocahontas-like.

The analysis of these different texts shows that there is a gap in this matter, that is, the need to establish a fixed identity that is not possible, and it is from this gap, according to Susan Scheckel, that the nation emerges, not as the coherent idea of a realistic narrative, but as an ongoing performance that continues to play out, "without resolution, [the] fundamental ambivalence of American national identity" (Scheckel 14). And in this ambivalent identity, the Pocahontas narratives play an important role.

NOTES

INTRODUCTION

[1] John Davis's *Travels of Four Years and a Half in the United States of America during 1798, 1799, 1800, 1801, and 1802* (1803) (259)

[2] Throughout this text, the people who lived in the American continent before the arrival of Europeans will be referred to either as "natives" in small font, or "Native Americans", in capitals. The term "Native American" is used instead of "Indians" except when quoting someone else, or between quotation marks when the use of this word is necessary. However, it is important to notice that both terms are misleading, as they imply a uniform population. The original inhabitants of the United States at the time of the European arrival belonged to hundreds of different tribes, with different languages and cultures. In fact, some of the tribes were constantly at war with

each other. Perhaps, it would be better to use the names they call themselves, like Lakota or Sioux, for example, but then it would be impossible to make any statement in which all would be included.

[3] Robert Tilton, *Pocahontas: the Evolution of an American Narrative* (Chapter 3, pages 58-92).

[4] Black Hawk, or Ma-ca-tai-me-she-kia-kiak, was an influential Sauk chief who took exception to an 1804 treaty, challenging its validity and disrespecting it. He was taken to prison and there he dictated his autobiography, which was edited by John B. Patterson and published in 1833 (Cheryl Walker *Indian Nation* 60).

[5] Although he does not use the expression "founding narrative", Slotkin emphasizes Cooper's importance among other American writers of the same period, stating that he is a "conscious artist" comparable to Hawthorne and Melville (467), aware of having created a myth. He also says that "Cooper's preeminence among mythologizers of the American frontier derives as much

from the manner in which he (and other artists of equal or greater power) approached the literary task as it does from his fortunate choice of subject matter." (468).

[6] For the purpose of this dissertation, I will use the expression "male centered texts" when referring to texts in which the main characters, the ones who really act and make decisions, are male, and the females are minor characters. "Female centered texts" are those with female as main characters, though they were not always able to decide for themselves, but the plot turned around them, and the main actions are also related to them.

[7] There is a strong connection between some of the liminal figures and the captivity among foreign people, for some of these liminal figures acquired their status after being abducted by the foreign people, no matter their race or gender. Such is the case of Pocahontas, Malinche and some other historical characters I have discussed in Chapter 3, sections 3.1. and 3.2.

[8] In *Farmer of New Jersey* (1800), a confused version of the story, "Smith is reduced to the rank of an Indian trader; Pocahontas is referred to at different junctures as a squaw and as an Indian queen; and the method of execution is altered from the clubbing described in Smith's account to burning at the stake" (William Warren Jenkins "The Princess Pocahontas and Three Englishmen Named John" 8). In *Travels of Four and a Half Years in the United States of America* (1803), Davis's earlier limited version of the Pocahontas story, referred to above, has grown into a thirty-seven page piece. Factual inaccuracies in the previous account were corrected, and details were amplified — part factual, part fictional. In *Captain Smith and the Princess Pocahontas: An Indian Tale*, and in *The First Settlers of Virginia*, both published in 1805, Davis tries to improve his previous treatment of the theme, but he was not successful, for "the action becomes increasingly bogged down in historical minutiae and geographical detail at the expense of that

sense of unity and aptness of tone which had made its shorter version in the *Travels* effective" (Jenkins 18). See the following chapter for a better discussion on the transformation of Pocahontas from a historical character into a fictional one.

[9] Boone is one of the most famous pioneers in United States history. He spent most of his life exploring and settling the American frontier. The legend of Daniel Boone was so glorified and manipulated throughout the 18th and 19th centuries that it is somewhat difficult to identify where the facts end and the myths begin. Boone's story was discovered and totally rewritten by the numerous "autobiographies" supposedly written and endorsed by Boone himself. In fact, Daniel Boone never wrote an autobiography. Matt Sparks, in "The Life and Legend of Daniel Boone", says that Boone was "barely literate and was infuriated by the manipulation of the facts of his life by these hagiographers. Boone actually wanted to sue his own nephew for publishing one of these

hagiographies" (1). John Filson's account of Boone, the first of these numerous "autobiographies", utilized his image as natural man to give authority to his story and to entice settlers to Kentucky — in essence, making Boone the ideal colonizer. In relation to the use of the Pocahontas narratives as sectionalist propaganda, see Robert Tilton's *Pocahontas: the Evolution of an American Narrative*, Chapter 5, 146-175.

[10] See Chapter 3 for a major discussion on her role as a mediator figure.

CHAPTER 1

[1] Thomas J. Wertenbaker, quoted in Frances Mossiker *Pocahontas, the Life and the Legend* 4

[2] William Byrd, *History of the Dividing Line Betwixt Virginia and North Carolina*[na 1.]

[3] Werowance is an Algonquian word meaning for chief or leader. Traditional Algonquian cultures were

highly matriarchal and women-centered in ways that European cultures were not. Thus, female werowance could be found sometimes ruling over small villages, all of them under the control of a more powerful male werowance.

[4] Although most of the Virginian texts were afterwards printed in the USA, their first editions were printed in London.

[5] Johann Fichte (1762-1814), German philosopher and educator, was the proponent of an idealist theory of reality and moral action based on will and ego. Although Fichte accepted most tenets of Kant's philosophy, he rejected Kant's theory of the unknowable 'things-in-itself' and his dichotomy between speculative and practical reason. His anonymously published essay *Critique of All Revelation* (1792) was at first thought to be the work of Kant. Fichte's other works include: *The Science of Knowledge* (1794); *The Science of Rights* (1796); and *The Science of Ethics as Based on the Science of Knowledge*

(1798). Fichte transformed Kant's critical idealism into an absolute idealism by making the ego and human will the ultimate reality. He held that the basis of all experience is the pure, spontaneous activity of the ego. All reality, according to Fichte, begins with the "transcendental ego" and is identifiable only through reflection upon primary experience. For Fichte, consciousness is a dynamic encounter between ego and non-ego in which the self and the world are interactively defined and realized. Fichte's ethical idealism, with its emphasis on moral will, derived in large part from these concepts. Fichte maintained that the world was created by an absolute ego, of which the human will is a partial manifestation, and which tends toward God as an unrealized ideal. He also held that philosophy must be based on science, developed systematically from a single self-evident proposition, to make clear the basis of all experience (Honderich 277-279)

[6] Friedrich Schelling (1775-1854) was another leading exponent of idealism and romanticism in German philosophy. His many works include: *The Philosophy of Art* (1807) and *Of Human Freedom* (1809). Schelling's early thinking was based chiefly on a close study (and synthesis) of Kant, Fichte, and Spinoza; from there Schelling's philosophy continually evolved. The distinguishing principle in his early work was the identity of subject and object, which became the basis of an identity philosophy that was generally pantheistic in nature, equating God with the forces and laws of the universe. Schelling went still further in reducing all reality to the self-realizing activity of an 'absolute spirit' which he identified with the creative impulse in nature. Later he rejected pantheism as too negative and developed what he called a positive philosophy in which he defined human existence as the mode of self-consciousness on the part of the Absolute. Schelling's emphasis on romanticism — on feeling and on the divinity of nature — later influenced

the American transcendentalist movement. (Honderich 800-801)

[7] Johann Gottfried Herder (1744-1803) was a German philosopher and literary critic whose work constitutes an important contribution to the early development of German Romanticism. As a part of that, he criticized the prevailing Enlightenment idea that the human faculty for reason could operate separately from the human passions and desires. He applied these ideas and more to his work on aesthetics, arguing that there is no such thing as an "innate" faculty of taste and that there are no objective, eternal standards of beauty. Instead, according to Herder, historical, cultural and psychological factors are what create distinct aesthetic standards which change over time. Herder was, thus, an early critic of the ideas of "timelessness" in art, a cause later taken up in postmodernism. (Honderich 352)

[8] Georg W.F. Hegel (1770-1831) was a German philosopher who, through his method of dialectical logic,

developed a philosophy of idealism centered on the concept of an Absolute. According to Hegel, human culture is actually just a manifestation of the self-consciousness of the Absolute. Indeed, he argued that the whole of reality was an expression of the Absolute, something he also called Absolute Spirit. Thus, he contradicted traditional Christian doctrine which held that God was separate and distinct from the universe. Instead, he argued that there wouldn't even be a God if there were not a universe through which God could be expressed. Because this fundamental principle is pure thought, Hegel's philosophy is a part of the tradition of idealism. Because this fundamental principle is a single substance, Hegel's philosophy is also a form of monism. (Honderich 339-342)

[9] Edmund Burke (1729-1797) was an Irish philosopher and statesman, remembered principally for his criticism of the French Revolution and his discussion of "the sublime". He was a founder of the Annual

Register and is regarded as the "father" of modern conservatism. Respected as a magnificent orator throughout his 30 year parliamentary career, Burke was often, perhaps unfairly, accused of inconsistency. He defended the English Revolution of 1688, and yet attacked the French Revolution bitterly. He was infuriated at the notion that Britain should learn from the French experience and allow all citizens the vote, and argued that traditional ruling practices in general and the monarchy in particular were essential elements of a stable, ordered society. Burke pitted the chaotic, uncontrollable changes of the French Revolution against (as he saw it) the British tradition of order and liberty. To Burke, the moral claim of the revolution to be in defense of the natural "rights of man" was a nonsense: although the British parliament depended on the approval of the British people for its authority to rule, this did not mean that citizens had the right to choose their rulers. Burke was a ruthless critic, however, of the excesses of established government: he campaigned against the persecution of Catholics in Ireland, denounced the East India Company and had the governor-general of Bengal impeached, and even expressed sympathy for the American Revolution. For Burke, there was no inconsistency in these views: it was the duty of citizens to submit to traditional authority, but it was equally the duty of rulers to act wisely and fairly. His strong criticism of the excesses of British rule in Ireland, India and America was not motivated by any wish to support the notion of natural rights; on the contrary, he argued, it was simple pragmatism: by ruling in a way that was manifestly unfair and exploitative, traditional authorities risked fomenting the worst of all possible outcomes, popular revolution. (Honderich 110-111)

[10] See Chapter 2 for a better discussion on nation and national identity.

[11] The notion that the Puritans were the founding fathers of the United States of America becomes really stronger after the Civil War (1861-1865), when the

Northern states won the war and established their hegemony over the country.

CHAPTER 2

[1] Homi K. Bhabha, "Introduction: narrating the nation" *Nation and Narration* 1.

[2] Henry Louis Gates Jr, *Loose Canons* 79.

[3] Gloria Anzaldúa, *Borderlands/La Frontera* 195.

[4] Mrs. Mary Rowlandson, *A Narrative of the Captivity and Restoration of Mrs. Mary Rowlandson by Herself.* (Dorson 235)

[5] Both Anderson and Bhabha base their argument on Renan's theory. Anderson, for instance, quotes Renan in *Imagined Communities* when explaining the need the nations feel to remember and/or forget certain events in order to build a national identity (199-201). Bhabha has translated Renan's text "Qu'est-ce une nation?", and included this article as the first one in Nation and

Narration. He also quotes Renan when discussing the need to forget and/or remember, when a nation is under construction (*Location of Culture* 161).

[6] "as identidades nacionais não são coisas com as quais nós nascemos, mas são formadas e transformadas no interior da representação" – my translation.

[7] "objetos privilegiados para a nova percepção que reduzia a humanidade a uma espécie, uma única evolução e uma possível perfectabilidade" – my translation.

[8] Thomas Jefferson, "Declaration of independence" (Bayn *et al* 294)

[9] The idea of a Chain of Being, or Scale of Creatures, is one of the guiding threads of interpretation of the universe worked out in Western science and philosophy. Like all ideas developed through a process of elaboration lasting centuries, it can be defined only by retracing its historical development in all its varied and often contradictory complexity. It will suffice to point out here what is constant in its many changing formulations.

The Chain of Being is the idea of the organic constitution of the universe as a series of links or gradations ordered in a hierarchy of creatures, from the lowest and most insignificant to the highest, indeed to the *ens perfectissimum* which, uncreated, is yet its culmination and the end to which all creation tends.

The conventionality of species is affirmed in Buffon's *Discours sur la manière d'étudier et de traiter l'Histoire naturelle*, which prefaces the first volume of his *Histoire naturelle* (1748). The methods or "systems" of classification are, to be sure, indispensable but artificial: as against the nuances of natural reality we have an arbitrarily articulated series. The error of all classification rests on the inability to grasp the processes of nature, which are always realized by degrees, by imperceptible nuances, thus escaping all division. In short, only individuals exist in reality; genera or species do not.

But Buffon wholly reversed his position in the course of his research, prompted by the now general recognition of species as a genetic entity. In fact, in Volume XIII of the same work (1765) he affirms that the only true beings in nature are species and *not* individuals. (*The Dictionary of the History of Ideas*<http://etext.lib.virginia.edu/cgi-local/DHI/dhi.cgi?id=dv1-31#>)

[10] Bhabha borrows the term from Freud, to whom "fetishism" is a form of paraphilia where the object of affection is an inanimate object or a specific part of a person.

[11] Squanto was a Wampanoag boy that was kidnapped as a child by some English traders, and bought by a Spanish monk, who treated him well and taught him the Christian faith. Afterwards, he came back to his land, and became an important figure for the Puritans, helping them several times. They then considered him as "God's special instrument".

[12] Slotkin here refers to the conception the English people had of themselves as the chosen people coming to a promised land.

CHAPTER 3

[1] Harris Patton, A. M., Patton, Jacob Harris. *The history of the United States of America, from the discovery of the continent to the close of the Thirty-sixth Congress* 50.

[2] Chapman, Jonson, and Marston. *Eastward Hoe. Representative English Comedies* 458.

[3] John Rolfe, "Letter to Governor Thomas Dale". Hamor 63. This quotation follows the original spelling of Rolfe's text, as written in 1613.

[4] Vachel Lyndsay, "Our Mother Pocahontas" *Collected Poems* 106.

[5] Archetype is the story that gives origin to others, the first one, and the origin of every story concerning a

certain aspect. Before Pocahontas, stories of maiden princesses saving the stranger already existed in Europe, as, for instance, the story of Ariadne and Theseus, from Greek Mythology. In the U.S.A., however, Pocahontas's story is the first.

[6] Even if the writers have not read Buffon's and/or de Pauw's theories, they were certainly aware of their existence, for such theories were widely spread throughout the country. And the way these writers portray the natives indicates that they were certainly aware of the ideas about racial superiority and the dangers of miscegenation appointed by those theories. See previous chapter, p. 56-57, for a brief discussion on such theories.

[7] This quotation follows the original spelling of Hamor's text as it was published in 1613.

[8] See Chapter 1 for a discussion on Robertson's text.

[9] Events similar to this one, in which a princess saves the life of a stranger, usually a prince, are frequently

found in fairy-tales, and the figure of Pocahontas has been many times compared to that of a fairy-tale princess. Marshall W. Fishwick, for instance, in *American Heroes, Myth and Reality*, points out that Pocahontas is "the fairy-tale princess come to life; a flesh-and-blood Cinderella in Indian disguise. Her story is full of romance and excitement" (35).

[10] This attitude of Pocahontas, of risking her life to save the life of the stranger, is also very common in fairy-tales. Maybe it was based on these kinds of texts, in which Pocahontas is like a fairy-tale princess, that the Disney Corporation released an animation supposedly based on her own life, but much closer to the fictional texts I have discussed in this dissertation than to the actual events of Pocahontas's life.

[11] I use the title bestowed on her by Barker as well as by some other authors, who applied European titles to Native Americans according to their status, without taking

into consideration the enormous cultural differences between the two peoples.

[12] I included this text to confirm my argument concerning the different treatment men and women received in relation to their attitudes, the white women's body being considered as legal property of their male relatives, fathers, brothers, or husbands.

[13] Powhatan was not only Pocahontas's father's name, but also the name of his people. Indeed, he was called Powhatan after his people, his actual name being Wahunsonacock (Swanton 66).

[14] William Wirt Henry, quoted by Abrams 249.

[15] Catherine Maria Sedgwick *Hope Leslie* 2:73

[16] Joel Barlow *Columbiad* 121.

[17] This may not be literally true, because many Spanish men had taken native women as mistresses. However, the idea of Malinche's son as the first mixed-blood child in present day Mexico is so well incorporated

in the legend of La Chingada that it is not possible to deny its importance.

[18] Iztaccihuatl was the daughter of an Aztec emperor in the Valley of Mexico. She had the misfortune of falling in love with one of her father's warriors. As soon as her father discovered their relationship, he sent her lover away to a war in Oaxaca. He told the young man that if he survived and returned he would give him Iztaccihuatl as his wife. The emperor never intended for the young warrior to return as he planned to marry Iztaccihuatl to another man. While her lover was away, Iztaccihuatl was told he was dead and she died of grief. Upon the young warrior's return, he took Iztaccihuatl's body in his arms and carried her to the mountains. He placed her on the ground and knelt beside her, dying of grief as well. The gods took pity on them, covering them with a blanket of snow and transforming them into mountains. Iztaccihuatl today is known as the "Sleeping Woman", as the mountain appears to be a woman lying on

her side. He became Popocatepetl, or "Smoking Mountain", the volcano that still rains down his revenge for the death of his lover (Narro 1-2)

[19] John Smith mixed first and third person narratives, a style Hulme calls "Caesarian third person" (3). That is why there are expressions like "our" and "we" in relation to the colonists, including himself, at the same time he refers to himself in the third person.

[20] Frances Mossiker, as well as other writers, like Robert Tilton and Peter Hulme, refers to the peaceful period from 1614 (year of her marriage) to 1622 (year of the massacre of Jamestown) as the "Peace of Pocahontas". In Mossiker's own words: "It was to be known as the Peace of Pocahontas. If it did not last forever, it lasted her lifetime" (183).

[21] In the case of Brazil, I am referring here to the mixed-blood people who were assimilated into white society, not to native people in themselves, whose

situation is still very complex and whose place in the Brazilian nation is still undetermined.

[22] Monique Mojica *Princess Pocahontas and the Blue Spots* 30.

[23] Charlotte Barnes *The Forest Princess* 342-343.

[24] The second type of narrative, usually fictional, is mostly based on the narratives of Pocahontas, especially after her story had been romanticized by John Davis.

[25] "City upon a Hill" is the name of a famous sermon preached by John Winthrop based on Matthew 5:14 ("You are the light of the world. A city set on a hill cannot be hid."), in which he urged that the Puritan colonists of New England who were to found the Massachusetts Bay Colony make their new community into a "city on a hill," an example to the Christian world.

[26] When Smith was a prisoner among the Turks (about 1601), he was sent to a noble lady, who fell in love with him and found a way not only to release him, but

also to save his life when her husband threatened to kill him (Warner 13).

CONCLUSION

[1] Monique Mojica *Princess Pocahontas and the Blue Spots* 31.

[2] Custalow-MacGowan. Quoted in Jacquelyn Kilpatrick "Disney's politically correct Pocahontas" 17.

[3] Hervey Allen. *New Legends, Poems* 127.

WORKS CITED

1. Primary Sources

Barker, James Nelson. *The Indian Princess; or, La Belle Sauvage*. Philadelphia, 1808. Jeffrey H. Richards, ed. *Early American Drama*. New York: Penguin, 1997.

Barnes, Charlotte. *The Forest Princess* (1848) In: Amelia Howe Kritzer, ed. *Plays by Early American Women, 1775-1850*. Michigan: University of Michigan Press, 1995. 321-368.

Child, Lydia Maria. *Hobomok* (1824). <http://etext.lib.virginia.edu/eaf>

Cooper, James Fenimore. *Notions of the Americans: Picked up by a Travelling Bachelor* (1828). New York: State University of New York, 1991.

---. *The Last of the Mohicans.* (1826). London: Penguin, 1994.

---. *The Pioneers.* (1823). New York: Signet Classic, 1964.

Custis, George Washington Parke. *Pocahontas, or The Settlers of Virginia.* Philadelphia, 1830. Arthur Hobson Quinn, ed. *Representative American Plays from 1767 to the Present.* New York: Appleton-Century-Crofts, 1917; rept. 1938.

Davis, John. *Travels of Four Years and a Half in the United States of America during 1798, 1799, 1800, 1801, and 1802.* London, New York, 1803.

Hamor, Ralph. *A True Discourse of the Present Estate of Virginia, and the successe of the affaires there till the 18 of Iune. 1614.* (1615) Albany: C. H. Barney, 1860.

Rolfe, John. "Letter to Governor Dale." Ralph Hamor. *A True Discourse of the Present Estate of Virginia, and the successe of the affaires there till the 18 of Iune. 1614.* (1615) Albany: C. H. Barney, 1860. 61-68

Sigourney, Lydia H. *Pocahontas and Other Poems*. New York: Harper and Brothers, 1841.

Sedgwick, Catherine Maria. *Hope Leslie* (1827). <http://etext.lib.virginia.edu/eaf>

Smith, John. *A True Relation of Such Occurrences and Accidents of Noate as Hath Hapned in Virginia ...* (1608). Philip Barbour, ed. *The Complete Works of Captain John Smith (1580-1631)*. Vol. 1. Chapel Hill: University of North Carolina Press, 1986.

---. *The Generall Historie of Virginia, New England and the Summer Isles ...* (1624). James MacLehose, ed. *The Travels of Captaine John Smith*. Vol. 1. New York: The Macmillan Company, 1907.

2. Secondary Sources

Abrams, Ann Uhry. "The Pocahontas Paradox: Southern Pride, Yankee Voyeurism, Ethnic Identity or Feminine

Heroics." Paper delivered at the annual meeting of the American Studies Association, October, 1988.

---, *The Pilgrims and Pocahontas: Rival Myths of American Origin.* Boulder: Westview Press, 1999.

Anderson, Benedict. *Imagined Communities.* London / New York: Verso, 1983; rept. 1991.

Allen, Theodore W. *The Invention of the White Race.* New York: Verso, 1994

Almeida, Sandra Regina Goulart. "Bodily Encounters: Gloria Anzaldúa's *Borderlands / La Frontera*". In: Anelise R. Corseuil, ed. *Ilha do Desterro.* N° 39. Florianópólis, SC: Jul/Dez 2000. 113-123.

Anzaldúa, Gloria. *Borderlands / La Frontera: the New Mestiza.* San Francisco: Aunt Lute, 1987.

Bancroft, George. *History of the United States of America, from the discovery of the American continent.* Boston: Little, Brown, and company, 1874-

78

Baker, Emerson W. *et al. American Beginnings: Exploration, Culture, and Cartography in the Land of Norumbega.* Lincoln, NE: University of Nebraska Press, 1994

Barlow, Joel. *The Columbiad; a poem.* London: R. Phillips, 1809.

Baym, Nina, *et al*, eds. *The Norton Anthology of American Literature.* 3 ed. New York / London: Norton & Company, 1989.

Beckson, Karl and Arthur Ganz. *Literary Terms.* 3 ed. New York: Noonday Press, 1989.

Bercovitch, Sacvan. *The Puritan Origins of the American Self.* New Haven and London: Yale University Press, 1975.

---, ed. *The Cambridge History of the American Literature.* New York & London: Yale University

Press.

Berkhofer, Robert, Jr. *The White Man's Indian*. New York: Random House, 1979.

Beverley, Robert. *The History and Present State of Virginia*. (1705). Richmond, VA: J. W. Randolph, 1855.

Bhabha, Homi K. *The Location of Culture*. New York: Routledge, 1994.

---, ed. *Nation and Narration*. New York: Routledge, 1990.

Bradbury, Malcolm and Richard Ruland. *From Puritanism to Post-Modernism*. London: Penguin, 1992.

Brown, Kathleen M. "Women in Early Jamestown" In: Crandall Shifflett, ed. *Jamestown Interpretive Essays*. 28 pars. 1999, 2000. (October 10th, 2003). http://www.iath.

virginia.edu/vcdh/jamestown/essays/brown_essay.htm l

Brydon, Diana. "'Empire bloomers'. Cross-dressing=s double cross." *Essays on Canadian Writing*. January, 1994. 50 pars. URL: http://www.elibrary.com. (June 14th, 1996).

Byrd, William. *History of the Dividing Line: Run in the Year 1728*. Petersburg, Va: Edmund and Julian C. Ruffin, 1841.

Campbell, Donna M. "Puritan Typology." *Literary Movements*. July 7, 2002, (November 11, 2002). http://www.gonzaga.edu/faculty/campbell/enl310/typo logy. htm.

Caspari, Rachel, and Milford Wolpoff. *Race and Human Evolution*. Boulder, CO: Westview Press, 1998.

Carignan, Michael I. "Fiction as History or History as Fiction? George Eliot, Hayden White and Nineteenth-

Century Historicism". *CLIO.* Vol. 29: 4, 2000. 395.

Chapman, George, Ben Jonson and John Marston. *Eastward Hoe* (1605). *Representative English Comedies: With Introductory Essays and Notes, an Historical View of Our Earlier Comedy.* Vol. 2. New York: The Macmillan Company, 1913.

Clay, Henry. "Seminole War". *Annals of Congress*, House of Representatives, 15th Congress, 2nd Session. http://memory.loc.gov/ammem/amlaw/lwac.html

Clinton, Catherine and Michele Gillespie, eds. *The Devil's Lane: Sex and Race in the Early South.* New York: Oxford University Press, 1997.

Cranston, Maurice. *The Romantic Movement.* Oxford UK & Cambridge USA: Blackwell, 1994.

Croly, David Goodman. *Miscegenation: the theory of the blending of the races, applied to the American white man and negro.* (New York, 1963); rept. London:

Trübner & Co., 1864.

Díaz del Castillo, Bernal. *The Discovery and Conquest of Mexico*. Translated and edited by A. P. Maudslay. New York: Farrar, Straus, and Giroux, 1956.

Dippie, Brian W. *The Vanishing American: White Attitudes and U.S. Indian Policy*. Middletown, Conn: Wesleyan University press, 1982.

Doren, Carl Van. *The American Novel*. New York: Macmillan, 1940.

Dorson, Richard M., ed. *America Begins*. Bloomington: Indiana University Press, 1971.

Drake, James D. *King Philip's War: Civil War in New England, 1675-1676*. Amherst: University of Massachusetts Press, 1999.

Elliot, Emory. "New England Puritan Literature". In: Sacvan Bercovitch, ed. *The Cambridge History of the American Literature*. New York & London: Yale

University Press, 1997.

Emerson, Ralph Waldo. *Nature* (1836). Nina Baym *et al*, eds. *The Norton Anthology of American Literature*. 3 ed. New York / London: Norton & Company, 1989. 384-412.

Faery, Rebecca Blevins. *Cartographies of Desire: Captivity, Race and Sex in the Shaping of an American Nation*. Norman, University of Oklahoma Press, 1999.

Fanon, Frantz. *The Wretched of the Earth*. New York: Grove Press, 1963.

Fiedler, Leslie. *The Return of the Vanishing American*. New York: Stein and Day Publishers, 1969.

Finkelman, Paul. "the Crime of Color". 67 *Tulane Law Review* (#6) 2063-2112 (June 1993) In: E. Nathaniel Gates, ed. *Racial Classification and History (Critical Race Theory: Essays on the Social Construction and*

Reproduction of "Race"). New York: Garland Publishing, 1997.

Fontaine, Peter. "Letter to Moses Fontaine, March 30, 1757". In: Ann Maury, *Memoirs of a Huguenot Family*. New York: Putman, 1872. 349

Fowler, David H. *Northern Attitudes toward Interracial Marriage*. New York: Garland, 1987.

Forrest, Tuomi. "Maid to Order: Columbus' 'Cannibal Girls' and the Captivity Narrative". In: *Pocahontas: Icon at the Crossroads of Race and Sex*. 8 pars. March 23rd, 2000. < http://xroads.virginia.edu/~CAP/POCA/POC-home.html>

Frankenberg, Ruth. *White Women, Race Matters: the Social Construction of Whiteness*. Minneapolis: University of Minnesota Press, 1993

Franklin, Benjamin. *Autobiography and Other Writings*.

Russel B. Nye, ed. Boston: Houghton Mifflin Company, 1958.

Gallagher, Edward J. "A Calendar of Pocahontas Materials" *The Pocahontas Archive*. (January 6th, 2001). <http://www.lehigh.edu/~ejg1/pocahontas/poca-cal.html>

Gans, Eric. "Originary Narrative". *Anthropoetics: The Electronic Journal of Generative Anthropology*. Vol. III, no. 2 (Fall 1997 / Winter 1998). 1-11. (September 6, 2004) <http://www.humnet.ucla.edu/humnet/anthropoetics/>

Germic, Stephen. "Border Crossing and the Nation: The Natural History of Nativ(ist) American Identity." Criticism. V. 42 N° 3 (Summer 2000) 337-57.

Gates Jr., Henry Louis. Loose *Canons: Notes on the Culture Wars*. New York: Oxford University Press, 1993.

Giddens, Sheshe. "The Development of *The Last of the Mohicans* as a Representation of a Normative American Romance" In: Craig White, ed. *American Romanticism*. 13 pars. Fall 2000. (October 25th, 2003) <http://coursesite.cl.uh.edu/HSH/Whitec /LITR/5535/models/2000/midterms/giddens.htm>

Gilroy, Paul. *Against Race: Imagining Political Culture Beyond the Color Line*. Cambridge: Harvard University Press, 2000.

Gonzalez, Barbara Renaud. "Pocahontas and her Sister Malinche". *Hispanic Link News Service* (1995). July 15th, 1996. <http://www.latinolink.com/his7233e.html>

Gossett, Thomas F. *Race: The History of an Idea in America*. New York: Oxford University Press, 1997.

Green, Rayna. "The Only Good Indian: The Image of the Indian in American Vernacular Culture." Ph.D. diss., Indiana University, 1973.

Hakluyt, Richard. *The Original Writings & Correspondence of the Two Richard Hakluyts*. vol. 76 and 77. London: The Hakluyt Society, 1935

Hall, Stuart. *A identidade Cultural Pós-Moderna*. Trad. Tomaz Tadeu da Silva & Cuaracira Lopes Louro, 4 ed. Rio de Janeiro: DP&A, 2000.

---. "Cultural Identity and Diaspora." Padmini Mongia, ed. *Contemporary Postcolonial Theory*. London: Arnold, 1996. 110-121.

Hamilton, Kendra. "Pocahontas: The Malleability of Race – or the Monster Miscegenation?" In: *Pocahontas: Icon at the Crossroads of Race and Sex*. 8 pars. March 23rd, 2000. < http://xroads.virginia.edu/~CAP/POCA/POC-home.html>

Hariot, Thomas. *A Briefe and True Report of the New Found Land Of Virginia*. (1590). Norman M. Wolcott, ed. July, 2003 [Etext# 4247].

Hening, William Waller. *The Statutes at large: Being a Collection of all the Laws of Virginia, from the First Session of the Legislature in the Year 1619.* New York: R & W & G. Bartow, 1823

Hickey, Donald R. *The War of 1812: a Forgotten Conflict.* Illinois: University of Illinois Press, 1990.

Hobsbawn, Eric and Terence Ranger, eds. *The Invention of Tradition.* Cambridge: Cambridge University press, 1983; rept. 1992.

Howe, Henry. *Historical Collections of Virginia . . .* Charleston, S.C.: W. R. Babcock, 1847.

Hulme, Peter. *Colonial Encounters: Europe and the native Caribbean, 1942 - 1797.* London and New York: Routledge, 1986. Rept. 1992.

Jefferson, Thomas. *Autobiography.* (1821) Electronic Text Center, University of Virginia Library. <http://etext.lib.virginia.edu/modeng/modengJ.browse

.html>

---. *Notes on the state of Virginia.* (1787) Electronic Text Center, University of Virginia Library http://etext.lib.virginia.edu/toc/modeng/public/JefVirg.html

---. *Writings of Thomas Jefferson.* Albert Ellery Bergh, ed. 19 vol. (1905). *Liberty Library of Constitutional Classics* <http://www.constitution.org/tj/jeff.htm>

Jehlen, Myra. "Why Did the Europeans Cross the Ocean? A Seventeenth-Century Riddle" Amy Kaplan and Donald E. Pease, ed. *Cultures of United States Imperialism.* Durham, NC.: Duke University Press, 1993. 41-58.

Jenkins, William Warren. "The Princess Pocahontas and Three Englishmen Named John." James W. Mathews, ed. *No Fairer Land: Studies in Southern Literature before 1900.* Troy, NY: Winston, 1986. 8-20.

Joseph, Beth. "Re(playing) Crusoe/Pocahontas: Circum-Atlantic Staging in *The Female American.*"(2000). 39 pars. May 10th, 2002. <http://www.findarticles.com>

Karttunen, Frances E. *Between Worlds: Interpreters, Guides, and Survivors.* New Brunswick, NJ: Rutgers University Press, 1994.

Kreis, Steven. "Toward a Definition of Romanticism." *The History Guide: Lectures on Modern European Intellectual History.* (2000). 9 pars. January 13th, 2002. <http://www.historyguide.org/intellect/romanticism.htm>

Kritzer, Amelia Howe, ed. *Plays by Early American Women, 1775-1850.* Michigan: University of Michigan Press, 1995.

Larson, Charles R. "Pocahontas animated." Vol. 11, *The World & I*, (02-01-1996): 28 pars. June 14th, 1996 < http://www.elibrary.com >

Lewis, Jone Johnson. "Women Captives and Indian Captivity Narratives: Stereotypes Reinforced and Challenged". *Women's History Guide*. 1999-2003. (November 8th, 2003). <http://womenshistory.about.com/library/weekly/aa02 0920a.htm>

Lindley, Susan Hill. *"You Have Stept out of Your Place": A History of Women and Religion in America*. Louisville, KY: Westminster John Knox Press, 1996

Lossing, Benson J., LL.D., "Our Country: Volume 1: Chapter XV." *U.S. History*, (09-01-1990): 36 pars. June 7th, 1996. <http://www.elibrary.com>

---, "Our Country: Volume 2: Chapter XXIV." *U.S. History*, (09-01-1990): 35 pars. June 7th, 1996. <http://www.elibrary.com>

MacDonald, Andrew and Maryann Sheridan. *Shape-Shifting: Images of Native Americans in Recent Popular Fiction*. Westport, CT: Greenwood Press,

2000.

MacGann, Jerome. *The Romantic Ideology*. Chicago: University of Chicago Press, 1983.

MacLehose, James, ed. *The Travels of Captaine John Smith*. Vol. 1. New York: The Macmillan Company, 1907

McFarland, Thomas. *Romanticism and the Heritage of Rousseau*. Oxford: Oxford University, 1995.

Marshall, John. *The Life of George Washington*. Vol. 1. New York: Wise, 1925.

Mahon, John K. *The War of 1812*. New York: Da Capo Press, 1991.

Mather, Cotton. *Magnalia Christi Americana*. (1668). 2 vol. Hartford: S. Andrus & son, 1853.

Mather, Cotton and Increase Mather. *Wonders of the Invisible World: Being an Account of the Tryals of Several Witches Lately Executed in New England*.

(1693). London: John Russell Smith, 1862.

Mojica, Monique. *Princess Pocahontas and the Blue Spots*. Toronto: Women=s Press, 1991; Rept. 1993.

Moody, Richard, ed. *Dramas from the American Theatre*, 1762-1909. Cleveland: World Publishing, 1966

Moraga, *Cherríe*. "From a Long Line of Vendidas: Chicanas and Feminism." De Lauretis, Teresa, ed. *Feminist Studies / Critical Studies*. Bloomington: Indiana University Press, 1986.

Mossiker, Frances. *Pocahontas, the life and the legend*. London: Gollancz, 1977.

Narro, Laura R. "Iztaccihuatl" M.F. Lindemans ed.. *Aztec mythology. Encyclopedia Mythica* (11 April 1999) November 6th, 2004. <http://www.pantheon.org/articles/i/ iztaccihuatl.html.>

Norton, Anne. *Reflections on Political Identity*. Baltimore,

Md.: John Hopkins University Press, 1988.

Peterson, Merrill D. *Thomas Jefferson and the New Nation: A Biography*. Oxford: Oxford University Press; New Ed edition, 1975.

Polino, Valerie Ann. "The Architecture of New England and the Southern Colonies as it Reflects the Changes in Colonial Life". In: *Colonial American History and Material Culture*, Volume IV, 1978.

Pratt, Mary Louise. *Imperial Eyes: Travel Writing and Transculturation*. London & New York: Routledge, 1992; rept. 1997.

Quinn, Arthur Hobson, ed. *Representative American Plays from 1767 to the Present*. New York: Appleton-Century-Crofts, 1917; rept. 1938

Quinn, David B. "The Early Cartography of Maine in the Setting of Early European Exploration of New England and the Maritimes." Emerson W. Baker *et al*, ed *American Beginnings: Exploration, Culture, and Cartography in the Land of Norumbega..* Lincoln, NE.: University of Nebraska Press, 1994. 37-59

Quinton, Anthony. "Romantic Irony". Ted Honderich, ed. *The Oxford Companion to Philosophy.* Oxford: Oxford University Press, 1995. 778.

---. "The Influence of Philosophy". Ted Honderich, ed. *The Oxford Companion to Philosophy.* Oxford: Oxford University Press, 1995. 672-73.

Rans, Geoffrey. *Cooper's Leather-Stocking Novels: A Secular Reading.* Chapel Hill, NC: University of North Carolina Press, 1991.

Rasmussen, William and Robert Tilton, *Pocahontas: Her Life and Legend*, Richmond: Virginia Historical Society, 1995.

Renan, Ernest. "What is a Nation?" Homi K. Bhabha, ed. *Nation and Narration.* New York: Routledge, 1990.

8-22.

Richards Jeffrey H., ed. *Early American Drama*. New York: Penguin, 1997.

Rissetto, Adriana. *Romancing the Indian: Sentimentalizing and Demonizing in Cooper and Twain*. (1996): 520 pars. April 5th, 2001 <http://xroads.virginia.edu/~HYPER/ HNS/Indians/main.html. >.

Robertson, Karen. "Pocahontas at the Masque." *Signs: Journal of Women in Culture and Society*. Los Angeles, CA, 1996. Spring; 21(3): 551-83.

Robertson, William. *The History of America*. Books IX and X. (1796) New York, Derby and Jackson, 1856.

Rousseau, Jean-Jacques. *The Social Contract and Discourses*. Trans. G. D. H. Cole New York : Dutton, 1950.

Rowlandson, Mary. *A Narrative of the Captivity and*

Restoration of Mrs. Mary Rowlandson by Herself. In: Richard M. Dorson, *America Begins*. Bloomington: Indiana University Press, 1971. 232-264.

Said, Edward. *Reflections on Exile and Other Essays.* Cambridge, Massachusetts: Harvard University Press, 2000.

Scheckel, Susan. *The Insistence of the Indian: Race and Nationalism in Nineteenth-Century American Culture.* Princeton: Princeton University Press, 1998.

Schülting, Sabine. "Bringing 'this monstrous birth to the world's light': Colonial mimicry in early modern writing". 45 pars. January 1996. <http://webdoc.gwdg.de/ edoc/ia/ eese/artic96/schulte/13_96.html>

Schwarcz, Lilia Moritz. *O Espetáculo das Raças: Cientistas, Instituições e questão racial no Brasil (1870 -1930).* São Paulo: Cia. Das Letras, 1993.

Shanahan, Daniel. *Toward a Genealogy of Individualism.* Amherst: University of Massachusetts Press, 1992

Simms, William Gilmore. *The life of Captain John Smith. The founder of Virginia.* 7th ed. Philadelphia: J.E. Potter & co., 1867.

Slotkin, Richard. *Regeneration Through Violence: The Mythology of the American Frontier, 1600-1860.* New York: Harper Perennial, 1996.

Sommer, Doris. *Foundational Fictions: The National Romances of Latin America.* Berkeley: University of California Press, 1991.

Smith, Anthony D. *National Identity: Ethnonationalism in Comparative Perspective.* Reno: University of Nevada Press, 1993

---. *Myths and Memories of the Nation.* New York: Oxford University, 1999.

Smith, David Nichol, *John Dryden.* Cambridge:

Cambridge University Press, 1950.

Smith, Harmon. *My Friend, My Friend: The Story of Thoreau's Relationship with Emerson*. Amherst, MA.: University of Massachusetts Press, 1999.

Spiller et alli, ed. *Literary History of the United States*. New York: Macmillan, 1974.

Spillman, Robert and Deborah Stein. *Poetry into Song: Performance and Analysis of Lieder*. New York: Oxford University Press, 1996.

Steele, Ian K *Warpaths: Invasions of North America*. New York: Oxford University Press, 1994.

Stith, William. *The History of the First Discovery and Settlement of Virginia*. (1747) Rept. New York, 1865 and Spartansburg, 1965.

Strachey, William. *The Historie of Travaile Into Virginia Britannia*. Ed. R. H. Major. London, 1849. (Written in 1612.) Louis B. Wright and Virginia Freund, eds.

London: Hakluyt Society, 1953.

Strong, Pauline Turner. *Captive Selves, Captivating Others: The Politics and Poetics of Colonial American Captivity Narratives.* Boulder, CO: Westview Press, 1999.

Tanrýsal, Meldan. "Squaws and Princesses or Corn Maidens: Misconceptions and Truths about Native American Women" In: Charles Brown, ed. *Native American Women.* (December 06th, 2000) <http://members.tripod.com/~warlight/MELDAN.html>

Taylor, Alan. "Fenimore Cooper's America". *History Today.* 46:2 (1996): 21+

Tilton, Robert S. *Pocahontas, the evolution of an American narrative.* Cambridge: Cambridge University Press, 1994.

Thompson, Benjamin. *New England's Crisis* (1676). In:

Kenneth Silverman, ed. *Colonial American Poetry.* New York: Hafner, 1968. 96-111.

Treece, David. *Exiles, Allies, Rebels: Brazil's Indianist Movement, Indigenist Politics, and the Imperial Nation-State.* Westport, CT: Greenwood Press, 2000.

Trinh, T. Minh-Ha. "Not You/Like You: Post-Colonial Women and the Interlocking Questions of Identity and Difference." In: Anne McClintock, Aamir Mufti, and Ella Shohat, eds., *Dangerous liaisons: gender, nation, and postcolonial perspectives.* Minneapolis : University of Minnesota Press, 1997. 415-419.

Unzueta, Fernando. "Novel Subjects: On Reading and National (Subject) Formations" *Chasqui.* 31: 2 (2002) . 75+.

Vaughan, Alden T. "People of Wonder: England Encounters the New World's Natives". Julie Ainsworth, Rachel Doggett, and Monique Hulvey, eds. *New World of Wonders: European Images of the*

Americas, 1492-1700. Washington, DC: The Folger Shakespeare Library, 1992. 11-23.

---. *Roots of American Racism: Essays on the Colonial Experience.* New York: Oxford University Press US, 1995.

---."Sir Walter Ralegh's Indian Interpreters, 1584 – 1618". *The William and Mary Quartely* 59.2 (2002): 55 pars. 30 Sep. 2002 ,http://www.historycooperative.org/journals/wm/59.2/vaughan.html>

Walker, Cheryl. *Indian Nation: Native American Literature and Nineteenth-Century Nationalisms.* Durham, NC: Duke University Press, 1997

Ward, Harry M. *The United Colonies of New England, 1643-90.* New York: Vantage Press, 1961.

Warner, Charles Dudley. *Captain John Smith.* Blackmask Online (2001), June 12th, 2002.

<www.blackmaslk.com>

Wasserman, Renata R. Mautner *Exotic Nations: Literature and Cultural identity in the United States and Brazil, 1830-1930.* Ithaca and London: Cornell University Press, 1994.

Webster, Noah. "History of Pocahontas." *An American Selection of Lessons in Reading and Speaking.* 12th edition. Hartford, 1797. 95-97.

Wertenbaker, Thomas J. *The Shaping of Colonial Virginia.* New York: Russell & Russell, 1958.

White, Hayden. *Tropics of Discourse: Essays in Cultural Criticism.* Baltimore & London: John Hopkins University Press, 1985.

Williams, Julie Hedgepeth. *The Significance of the Printed Word in Early America: Colonists' Thoughts on the Role of the Press.* Westport, CT:Greenwood Press, 1999.

Winkfield, Unca Eliza. *The Female American, or, The Adventures of Unca Eliza Winkfield.* (1767). (Rptd. as *The Female American, or, The Extraordinary Adventures of Unca Eliza Winkfield* or *The Female American* in 1800, 1814, 1970, 1974) New York: Broadview Press, 2000.

WORKS CONSULTED

Aidman, Amy. "Disney's Pocahontas: Conversations with Native American and Euro-American Girls". Sharon R Mazzarella and Norma Odom Pecora, eds. *Growing Up Girls: Popular Culture and the Construction of Identity.* New York: Peter Lang, 1999 133-158.

Ainsworth, Julie, Rachel Doggett and Monique Hulvey, eds. *New World of Wonders: European Images of the Americas, 1492-1700.* Washington, DC: The Folger Shakespeare Library, British Library, 1992.

Allen, Paula Gunn. "Pocahontas to her English Husband John Rolfe". In: Jerome Beaty and J. Paul Hunter, ed. *New Worlds of Literature.* New York: W.W. Norton, 1989. 813-14

Allen, Robert C. *Horrible Prettiness: Burlesque and American Culture* Chapel Hill, NC: University of North Carolina Press, 1991.

Belknap, Jeremy. *American Biography.* Vol. 1. Boston, 1794.

Bellei, Sérgio Luís Prado. "Uma história mal contada: Pocahontas and John Smith" Centro Regional de Estudios sobre Estados Unidos. *De Sur a Norte: Perspectivas Sudamericanas sobre Estados Unidos.* Vol. 3. N. 4. Universidade de Palermo, Argentina. Abril 1998. (129-150)

Bradbury, Malcolm and Howard Temperley, eds. *Introduction to American Studies.* London/New York: Longman, 1989.

Carvalho, Humberto C. *Fundamentos de Genética e Evolução.* 3 ed. Rio de Janeiro / São Paulo: Atheneu, 1987.

Cook-Lynn, Elizabeth. "American Indian Intellectualism and the New Indian Story (Writing about American Indians)". Devon A. Mihesuah, ed. *Natives and Academics Researching and Writing about American*

Indians University of Nebraska Press; (April 1, 1998). 111-138

Degler, Carl. *Out of Our Past*. New York: Harper Books, 1970.

Elson, Henry William. *History of the United States of America*. New York: The MacMillan Company, 1904.

Everett, William A. and Peter Arnds. "Manifestations of Folk and Fairy Tales in 19th- and 20th-*century* Literature< theatre, Music and Art." Odd-Bjørn Fure, ed. *European Identity and its Expression in Philosophy, Science, Literature and Art*. Norway: University of Bergen. (2000) 3 pars. January 16th, 2002. <http://www.uib/issei2000/workshop/sec.4/everett.htm>

Fanon, Frantz. Black *Skins, White Masks* .New York: Grove Press, 1967.

Gayley, Charles Mills, ed. *Representative English*

Comedies: With Introductory Essays and Notes, an Historical View of Our Earlier Comedy. Vol. 2. New York: The Macmillan Company, 1913.

Crasnow, Ellman and Philip Haffenden. "New Founde Land." Malcolm Bradbury and Howard Temperley, eds. *Introduction to American Studies.* London/New York: Longman, 1989. 31-55.

Guglielmo, Antônio Roberto. *A Pré-História: uma abordagem ecológica.* São Paulo: Brasiliense, 1999.

Hampson, Thomas and Carla Maria Verdino-Süllwold. "Romanticism." *I Hear America Singing on the Web.* (2000). 6 pars. January 12th, 2002. http://www.pbs.org/wnet/ ihas/icon/romanticism.html

Jarman, Catherine. *Evolução da Vida.* Trans. Mathilde Mona Cohen. São Paulo: Melhoramentos, 1978.

Kroeber, Karl, ed. *Studies in American Indian Literature.* Vol.11. N. 1. Columbia University, New York,

Winter 1987.

Lewin, Roger. *Evolução Humana*. Trans. Danusa Munford. São Paulo: Atheneu, 1999.

Lima, Celso Piedemonte de. *Evolução Humana*. São Paulo: Ática, 1990.

Lipson, Karin. "'Pocahontas': Just Whose History Is It?" *Newsday*. (06-20-1995): June 14th, 1996. < http://www.elibrary.com. >

Locke, John. *An Essay Concerning Human Understanding*. (1690). 1644 pars. October 24th, 2003. <http://www.ilt.columbia.edu/publications/locke_understanding.html>

Mazzarella, Sharon R and Norma Odom Pecora, eds. *Growing Up Girls: Popular Culture and the Construction of Identity*. New York: Peter Lang, 1999.

Milanich, Jerald T. and Susan Milbrath, eds. *First Encounters: Spanish Explorations in the Caribbean and the United States, 1492-1570*. Gainesville, FL: University of Florida Press, 1989.

Moffitt, John F. and Santiago Sebastián. *O Brave New People: The European Invention of the American Indian*. Albuquerque: University of New Mexico Press, 1996

Montalenti, Giuseppe. *Introdução à Biologia*. Trans. Eduardo Saló. Lisbos: Notícias, s.d.

Pope, Alexander. *The works of Alexander Pope ... With notes by Dr. Warburton, and ilustrations on steel by eminent artists*. From designs by Weigall, Heath, & others. Philadelphia: W. P. Hazard, 1856.

Richardson, Edgar P. American Romantic Painting. Robert Freund, ed. New York: E. Weyhe, 1944.

Said, Edward. *Culture and Imperialism*. New York:

Vintage Books, 1993.

---, *Orientalism*. New York: Pantheon, 1978.

Sayre, Gordon M. *Les Sauvages Americains: Representations of Native Americans in French and English Colonial Literature*. Chapel Hill, NC: University of North Carolina Press, 1997.

Sinclair, Abiola. "Media Watch: The Real Pocahontas, Part II" *New York Amsterdam News*. (07-22-1995): 113 pars. June 12th, 1996. < http://www.elibrary.com. >

Sparks, Matt. "The Life and Legend of Daniel Boone." *Historical Context* (2000). April 10th, 2003. <http://www.lehigh.edu/~ineng/mrs6/mrs6-historicalcontext.html>

Schwarcz, Lilia Moritz e Renato da Silva Queiroz. *Raça e Diversidade*. São Paulo: EDUSP, 1996.

Smith, Henry Nash. *Virgin Land: The American West as*

Symbol and Myth. Cambridge, Massachusetts: Harvard University Press, 1950; rept. 1978.

Strickland, Brad. "American Literary Romanticism: History." (1997). Unpublished Material. 7 pars. January 13th, 2002. <http://troy.gc.peachnet.edu/www/bstrickl/lit/history.htm>

Strong, Pauline Turner. "Review on Disney's Pocahontas." *H-Women - H-Net Reviews in the Humanities and Social Sciences*. (July, 1995) 26 pars. August 5th, 1996 <http://www2.h-net.msu.edu/mmreviews/ showrev.cgi?path=41>

Swanton, John R *The Indian Tribes of North America*. Washington, DC: U.S. Government Printing Office, 1952.

Vickers, Scott B. *Native American Identities: From Stereotype to Archetype in Art and Literature*. Albuquerque, NM: University of New Mexico Press,

1998.

Woodlief, Ann. "Introduction." *American Romanticism / American Renaissance*. (June 2000). 15 pars. August 15th, 2002. <http://www.vcu.edu/engweb/eng372/intro.html>

Young, Philip. "The Mother of Us All: Pocahontas reconsidered." The Kenyon Review. Vol. XXIV, N. 3. Summer 1962. (391-415)

www.ingramcontent.com/pod-product-compliance
Lightning Source LLC
Chambersburg PA
CBHW022056090426
42743CB00008B/626